Table Tennis Tactics—Be A Successful Player

ACKNOWLEDGMENT, OR (TO QUOTE JOE COCKER) "WITH A LITTLE HELP FROM OUR FRIENDS"

The authors thank:

The Butterfly company for their support.

Timo Boll for his friendly and very professional collaboration on the photo shoots.

*Guido Schuchert for the great photos,
without which our book would not have been so well illustrated.*

*Oliver Sprigade for preparing the images. He had the difficult task
of representing what we were not able to communicate via photos
or the written word. He is also the creator of the 'tactical fox.'*

Another big THANK YOU to all those mentioned above.

Klaus-M. Geske & Jens Mueller

TABLE TENNIS *TACTICS*

Be A Successful Player

Meyer & Meyer Sport

Original title: Tischtennistaktik
© Meyer & Meyer Verlag, 2009

Translation: Heather Ross & AAA Translation, St. Louis, Missouri

British Library Cataloguing in Publication Data
A catalogue record for this book is available from the British Library

Table Tennis Tactics. Be A Successful Player

Klaus-M. Geske & Jens Mueller

Maidenhead: Meyer & Meyer Sport (UK) Ltd., 2017

ISBN: 978-1-78255-112-6

© 2017 by Meyer & Meyer Sport (UK) Ltd.

2nd revised edition

Auckland, Beirut, Dubai, Hägendorf, Hong Kong, Indianapolis, Cairo, Cape Town,

Manila, Maidenhead, New Delhi, Singapore, Sydney, Teheran, Vienna

Member of the World Sports Publishers' Association (WSPA)

www.w-s-p-a.org

Printed by: Print Consult GmbH, Munich, Germany

ISBN: 978-1-78255-112-6

E-mail: info@m-m-sports.com

CONTENTS

GREETING FROM TIMO BOLL

Hi there!

Do you enjoy table tennis as much as I do? I hope so, for it is certainly one of the fastest, most exciting and diverse sports around. It can be rather confusing though, if, for example, you are only able to return serves high, if at all, or still haven't understood how to play against different types of table tennis rubbers.

In case you have ever wondered why a coach advised you to play more on the forehand side against one opponent but the opposite against another, the many explanations and tips contained in this book will give you some suggestions to help your game.

I hope you have fun and find the answers to your unresolved questions! And if you feel like seeing great players in action, why not attend a National League game?

Bye for now!

Timo

FOREWORD

Do you know this feeling? You have just lost to a player and even after the game you thought that you were the better player.

What makes you think that?

Perhaps his technique is not as elegant as yours in the most important stroke, the forehand topspin? Or did you only lose because you couldn't control your returns of serve? "But otherwise" you may now add "I was much better at him at everything!"

Is that really true?

Let us first consider what elements a good table tennis player needs.

The first is technique, for after all, that is that is practiced the most (e.g. with many-balls-training).

Another component is definitely fitness (also called conditioning). This is made up of the five areas of speed, coordination, flexibility, endurance and strength that every player needs.

Is it also important to be able to keep your nerve in table tennis? We think so. For what use is all your ability if you can never play your best in a match due to nerves? We are talking about the typical *training world champion*.

It is expressed by rushing about too hectically during rallies, which causes you to make unforced errors or prevents you from making the most of your chances, and by literally standing like a rabbit in front of a snake, being so tense that your actions run in slow motion and are easy for the opponent to anticipate.

Boris Becker, the German tennis player and two-times Wimbledon champion, once said: "Today I was not all there mentally."

This brings us to the fourth component, which forms the subject of this book: tactics.

We do not intend to simply tell you how to play against certain types of players. The aim of this book is to teach you to automatically implement the tactics learned in training in matches, and with this in mind, we have added a drills section with many training tips at the end of each of the five main chapters.

Let us return to the opening question.

We don't play table tennis to demonstrate textbook technique but to win, for which good technique is essential.

But in our opinion, many coaches and trainers place too much emphasis on perfecting the hitting techniques instead of showing how and when they can be used to win points.

This requires a certain theoretical background. One must learn to understand the game of table tennis. But this kind of table tennis lesson is hard to find.

We decided to write this book in order to give ambitious up-and-coming players a helping hand.

We have tried to explain quite complicated topics as simply as possible, by including many photos and illustrations in order to aid understanding of the text. The five *tactical foxes* provide valuable tips and advice throughout the book.

Committed coaches and trainers can also use the graphics and illustrations as source material for theory classes, which, in our opinion, should be an indispensable part of table tennis training.

We hope you enjoy reading this book and wish you well on *your personal path to success*!

Hanover and Meerbusch, Germany

Klaus-M. Geske and Jens Mueller

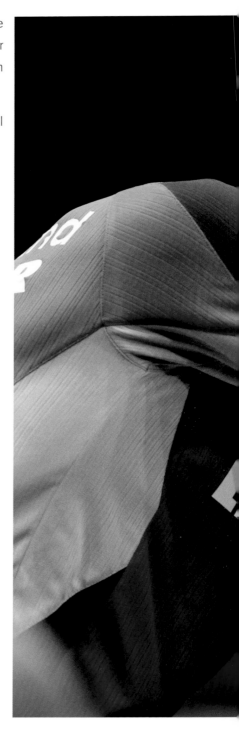

BEFORE WE START, JUST A FEW MORE TIPS:

Our descriptions are limited to right-handed players for the sake of simplicity.

If you are a left-handed player, just reverse the description where necessary, which shouldn't be too hard! For example, if the text says play further to the right on the forehand side, for the left-handed player this means exactly the opposite, i.e. play further to the left on your forehand side!

When we talk about hitting a ball cross-court, this means hitting it from forehand side to forehand side in the case of two right-handers.

If we suggest you play parallel, you must hit the ball almost straight ahead from whichever position you are in, i.e. in the above-mentioned case of two right-handers, this would be from your forehand side to the opponent's backhand side!

In the drills section at the end of each chapter, you will often see the phrase: "serve short over the whole table." By this we mean that you can serve the ball where you like as long as you play it short.

Many drills end in free play. This means after a few predefined strokes, you and the partner with whom you are practicing the drill play for points!

This makes the drill match-specific. While you play the drills that do not culminate in free play with each other, in the drills that do culminate in free play, you play against each other. In free play, your partner becomes your opponent.

Even if a drill mentions "play a short serve," you should also throw in a long serve from time to time for an element of surprise so that your partner does not get too used to short serves and stands right next to the table to return serve so as not to have to move around too much. As soon as you notice this happening, you should shake things up a bit with a long ball. Remember to do this in competitions too!

Of course, the same applies to the receiver, who, although he could play, for example, a long forehand return, decides to play a short drop shot in order to vary his game.

At the same time, this interspersing of surprise shots draws on your creativity and powers of observation!

In the drills sections we use the usual abbreviations FH and BH for the terms forehand and backhand.

Throughout the book we use the term "racket," which is also referred to as a "paddle" in the USA.

For the sake of simplicity, we use only the masculine form of address; it goes without saying that this refers to both men and women.

BALL PLACEMENT

01

1 BALL PLACEMENT

In our first chapter we want to show how important it is to position your shots correctly on the opponent's side of the table. For orientation, we use two different zone divisions for the table. In the first zone division, one half of the table is subdivided into three zones:

- The **net zone**
- The **middle zone**
- The **baseline zone**

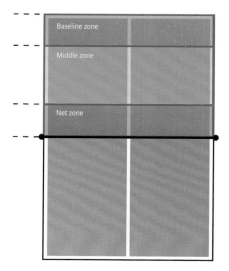

Fig. 1 First zone division of the table.

As this division is still quite rough, we would like to present a second option, in which half of the table is divided into four areas (from left to right):

- **Wide forehand**
- **Forehand area**
- **Backhand area**
- **Wide backhand**

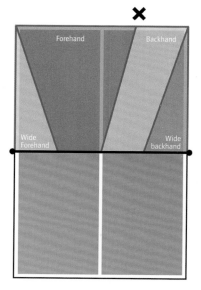

Fig. 2: Second zone division of the table.

The four areas are completed by the 'elbow' position (see black cross), which is explained in more detail in section 1.1. The two table divisions shown complement each other very well as they allow ball placements to be described more accurately, e.g. "long (baseline zone) in the deep forehand."

WHY IS IT SO IMPORTANT?

It should help you to observe your opponent more consciously in order to identify his strengths and weaknesses. For example, if you play a FH topspin to his FH side, you should consider beforehand whether your opponent blocks better with his FH or BH side and then of course hit more often to his weaker side. You are also more able to discuss with your coach before a competition if you use the same technical terms and avoid unnecessary misunderstandings.

WHICH ARE THE BEST TECHNIQUES
TO USE WHEN HITTING TO THE DIFFERENT ZONES?

The **net zone** can be targeted with short serves, push balls or dropshots. A ball is considered to be short if it bounces at least twice on the opponent's side of the table—assuming of course that it is allowed to bounce and is not returned.

The **middle zone** should if possible only be targeted in the far forehand or backhand sides, and by shots for which the opponent cannot be absolutely sure whether the ball could bounce twice or is long, i.e. would land beyond the table. Other placements in the middle zone should not be attempted because they are usually very easy for your opponent to return.

The **baseline zone** should be aimed for when hitting a wide forehand or backhand and the 'elbow' placement, for it is hard for the opponent to return balls hit to these places. You can hit them with any stroke except short push balls and drop shots.

Your topspin, in particular, becomes much more dangerous when you hit it as long as possible (into the baseline zone)!

1.1   ELBOW

You should definitely consider hitting to thisarea, as it can cause big problems for your opponent!

The *elbow* is the point at which a player with a shake-hand grip (see section 1.3) must decide whether to return the ball with a forehand or a backhand.

As this decision must often be taken under great time pressure and usually means that the player must take a step to the side in order to be in the right position to hit the ball, this placement presents problems for bigger and less agile players.

However, remember that this point varies according to the player's position to the table, which also changes frequently during rallies.

The elbow point shifts further and further to the right (to the forehand side) the shorter the incoming ball bounces and is hit, because the backhand side has greater range and agility, particularly in the mid-table area.

Further information on the topic of playing 'elbow' can be found in this chapter under the points 1.4.1 and 1.4.2 'Characteristics of forehand and backhand dominant players.'

Photo 2

Photo 1

How the *elbow* point shifts to the forehand side in the case of short balls.

Photo 3

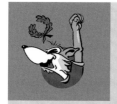 *It is particularly advisable to play 'elbow' against good blocking players who are solid on both the forehand and backhand sides! But also a well-placed push or block to the elbow can put even world class players like Timo under great pressure (see photos 4 and 5!).*

Photo 4

Photo 5

1.2 SCATTERING ANGLE

Have you ever noticed that by changing the placement of your shots, the placement possibilities for your opponent's backhands change also?

All the possible placements from a given hitting point are represented by the scattering angle, and every hitting point has a **scattering angle**.

Don't worry, it sounds more complicated than it is!

By way of illustration, we show the following scattering angles for the hitting points:

- Long to wide forehand
- Long to wide backhand
- Long to the center of the table
- Short to the center of the table

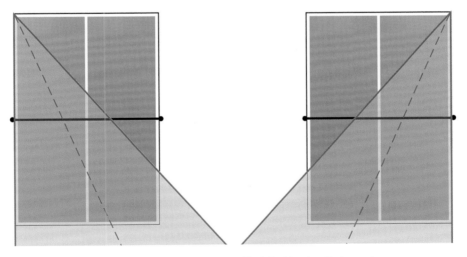

Fig. 3: Forehand scattering angle   Fig. 4: Backhand scattering angle

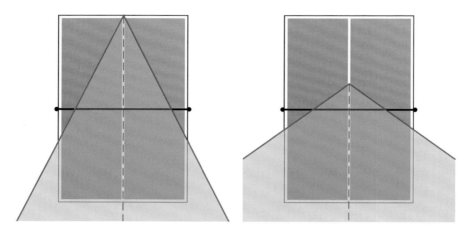

Fig. 5: Scattering angle long down the center of the table

Fig. 6: Scattering angle short down the center of the table

1.2.1   IMPLICATIONS FOR TRAINING AND COMPETITION

CASE 1:

If you hit a ball long into the wide forehand (see fig. 3), your opponent can play a completely parallel return into your deep backhand. Or, cross-court, he can play a return shot very wide to your forehand side.

IMPLICATION:

In order to be able to cover your forehand side adequately for the opponent's next shot, change your position to the table to the backhand side!

CASE 2:

If, on the other hand, you hit a ball long into the wide backhand (see fig. 4), your opponent can play a totally parallel return to your deep forehand. Or, cross-court he can hit his shot very wide to your backhand side. Your opponent's placement possibilities are exactly the opposite of those in case 1.

IMPLICATION:

In order to be able to cover your backhand side adequately for your opponent's next shot, alter your position to the table, i.e. to the backhand side!

CASE 3:

A ball placed long in the center of the table (see fig. 5) can be returned as a deep cross-court shot by your opponent equally well to your forehand or backhand sides. Make sure that, unlike cases 1 and 2, he is not able to place the ball so wide cross-court.

IMPLICATION:

In order to be equally well-prepared for your opponent's return on the forehand or backhand sides, you should position yourself to the table so that your racket is situated at the point that bisects the scattering angle (see dotted line = the halfway line)!

1.2.2 CONCLUSION

Every time you play a shot, make sure that you are ready to receive your opponent's return holding your racket at the point that bisects the scattering angle!

This means that you reduce your running to a minimum and are able to cover both sides of your half of the table equally well. Jan-Ove Waldner and Vladimir Samsonov are two world-class players who use this principle to the best effect during matches. As they make the best use of the time between shots to prepare for the next shot, they are much less subject to time pressure than other players, which in turn leads to a calmer and more error-free game.

Don't waste time after a shot by just watching the ball to check that it bounces on your opponent's half of the table! Instead, prepare for your next shot while watching where the ball lands!

Move towards the line that bisects the scattering angle until you have reached it, or until you can see where the opponent is going to hit his return!

1.2.3   A BRIEF GLANCE BEYOND OUR SPORT

You can see how this is put into practice during baseline rallies in tennis on the television. Compared to table tennis, tennis players have to run further, but there is more time to do this between strokes.

If a player receives a shot deep into one corner, he first moves into the relevant corner, then plays his shot and is already on his way back to the center of the court before the ball bounces in the opponent's court.

If he had remained in that corner, the opponent could easily have played a winning return into the opposite corner with his next shot.

What in tennis is considered natural, as longer running paths caused by bad positioning are immediately obvious and cause errors, is still all too often neglected in table tennis or simply not noticed.

Although the running paths in our sport are shorter than in tennis, there is also less time available to cover them!

1.3 RACKET GRIP

For the former Swedish national coach Glenn Östh (men's team world champion in 1989), the racket grip has the biggest influence on a player's technical possibilities. He refers to the most widely found grip in Europe, the so-called **shake-hand grip**. This grip can be divided into three different types:

NEUTRAL GRIP:

The upper edge of the racket blade forms an exact extension of the fold of skin formed when the thumb and index finger of the outstretched hand move together.

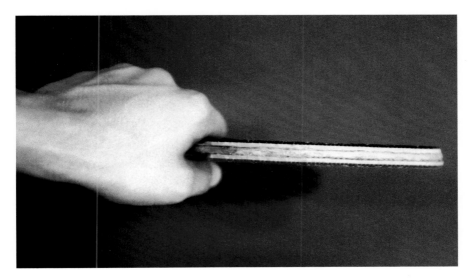

Photo 6

The neutral grip offers equal wrist mobility for both forehands and backhands, and can be used for all strokes.

FOREHAND GRIP

The racket blade is tilted towards the thumb. This grip is characterized by increased freedom of movement on the forehand side compared to the neutral grip, and is therefore particularly suited to forehand strokes, hence its name. On the backhand side though, there is less freedom of movement than with the neutral grip, so it is less suited to most backhand strokes.

Photo 7

BACKHAND GRIP

Here the racket blade is tilted towards the index finger. This grip gives greater freedom of movement on the backhand side than the neutral grip, and is therefore particularly suited to backhand strokes, as the name suggests.

It is less suited to forehand strokes as there is less freedom of movement compared to the neutral grip.

As well as these three grips there are countless others such as the extreme forehand and extreme backhand grips, which have added advantages but also added disadvantages! Östh & Fellke also point out another grip-related aspect:

"Where the player grips the racket is also important. Players who hold the racket very high (i.e. very near the blade and the rubbers), such as 1985 double world champion, Ulf Carlsson, obtain good stability and good force development in strokes that require a long backswing and follow through, but wrist movements are greatly restricted, particularly for short play. A lower grip (i.e. right at the bottom of the racket), as favored by Jörgen Persson, shifts the center of gravity of the racket and reduces the player's control of the racket during long movements. Wrist mobility is good, which is enormously advantageous for serving and play directly behind the net."

Photo 8

1.3.1   THE GRIP TABLE ACCORDING TO ÖSTH/FELLKE

The table below was compiled by the previously mentioned Swedish coach Glenn Östh and Jens Fellke, a former Swedish first division player. It shows which grips are advantageous for which strokes and side changes. For example, a FH topspin is easier with the forehand grip while the backhand grip is helpful for a FH-sidespin. They also indicate that by changing grip (also known as 'flipping the racket') during a rally, it is possible to change the grip in order to play as many strokes as possible with good technique.

Strokes	Grip
FH-topspin	FH-grip
BH-topspin	BH-grip
FH-smash	BH-grip
BH-smash	FH-grip
FH-flip	FH-grip
BH-flip	BH-grip
Quick change from FH to BH	BH-grip
Quick change from BH to FH	FH-grip
FH parallel from the FH corner	FH-grip
BH parallel from the FH corner	BH-grip
FH cross-court from the FH corner	BH-grip
BH cross-court from the BH corner	FH-grip
FH from mid-table	FH-grip
BH from mid-table	BH-grip
FH sidespin	BH-grip
Defensive FH chop	BH-grip
Defensive BH chop	FH-grip

Fig. 7

1.3.2   IMPLICATIONS FOR TRAINING AND COMPETITION

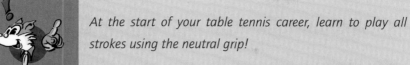

At the start of your table tennis career, learn to play all strokes using the neutral grip!

Deliberately avoid changing grip as mentioned above during rallies as it is too demanding for novices!

Your basic training is completed when you confidently master the different strokes and start to develop your own game. In this phase it is a good idea to experiment to see whether grip changing improves your game, particularly in your favored strokes. Should this not be the case, stick with the less risky neutral grip!

As well as thinking about your own grip, don't forget to also keep an eye on your opponent's!

By identifying his preferred grip, particularly when he doesn't flip, you will know which strokes will be easy or difficult for him to play. Knowledge of Östh & Fellke's grip table helps you to play deliberately to his grip-related weak spots. It also tells you which strokes you should let him play the least, as they are probably his strongest weapons.

In the next section we present the two types of game that are most widespread. You will notice that the knowledge of the grips helps you to understand the typical strengths and weaknesses of both types of game.

1.4   GAME TYPES

1.4.1   CHARACTERISTICS OF A FOREHAND-DOMINANT PLAYER

A forehand-dominant player tries to play as many shots as possible with his stronger forehand, hence the name.

For this reason, he runs around his weaker backhand side at every available opportunity.

You can spot a typical forehand-dominant player (right-hander) by the following four characteristics:

Grip: The racket is usually held with a forehand grip!

Foot position: The right foot is usually well behind the left!

Position to the table: The player stands on the backhand side!

Elbow: The 'elbow' point is more on the backhand side! This means that the forehand-dominant player's elbow is usually on the left near the point that bisects the scattering angle, as he is trying to cover as much of the table as possible with his forehand.

Remember that Timo is left-handed, so reverse the actions for a right-handed player!

Photo 9a   Photo 9b

1.4.1.1   TIPS FOR PLAYING AGAINST A FOREHAND-DOMINANT PLAYER

The characteristics described above mean that the following are weak spots for the forehand-dominant player, and should be played to as often as possible:

- *Long into the wide forehand and backhand sides!*
- *Short into the wide forehand side!*

The forehand-dominant player will find it very difficult to play an effective forehand return in these cases, as he must move wide and is often forced to return with his weaker backhand side.

NOTE:

It may at first seem illogical to play to the forehand side of a player with a very strong forehand, but remember that this placement stops the forehand player from running around his backhand side, which is his specialty after all.

You should therefore be aware not only of your opponent's most dangerous strokes but also the position he plays them from!

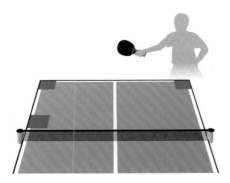

Fig. 8: Weak spots
of the forehand-dominant player.

Photo 10

Photo 11

Photo 12

As always, the actions should be reversed for left-handed players!

Here, Timo shows the weak spots of a forehand-dominant left-hander!

1.4.2   CHARACTERISTICS OF A BACKHAND-DOMINANT PLAYER

A backhand-dominant player only rarely runs around his backhand side and prefers to return mid-table balls with his stronger backhand side. You can recognize a typical backhand-dominant player by the following four characteristics:

Grip: The racket is usually held with a backhand grip!

Foot position: The feet are parallel to, and the same distance away from, the table!

Position to the table: The player stands approximately in the center of the table!

Elbow: The elbow point tends to be situated more on the forehand side! This means that the backhand-dominant player's elbow is usually on the right near the bisection of the scattering angle because he tries to cover his backhand side and as much of the table as possible with his backhand.

Photo 13

1.4.2.1   TIPS FOR PLAYING AGAINST BACKHAND-DOMINANT PLAYERS

The characteristics described above mean that the following are weak spots for the backhand-dominant player, and should be played to as often as possible:

- *Long down the elbow and then wide on the backhand side!*
- *Short on the forehand side and on the elbow!*

The backhand-dominant player has great trouble with balls hit to his elbow as this forces him to open his backhand side, making him very vulnerable to a ball on the wide backhand.

Make sure that the elbow point for short balls is situated further to the forehand side than for long balls!

The former coach of the German National women's team, Martin Adomeit, also points out that increased stress during matches causes the elbow point to shift even further to the forehand side.

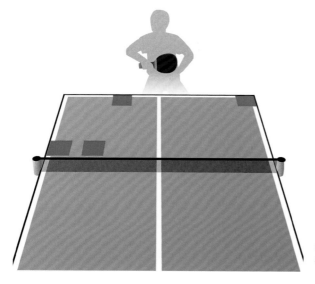

Fig. 9: Weak spots of the backhand-dominant player

The backhand grip also makes it hard for the backhand-dominant player to flip well with the forehand as the freedom of movement is greatly reduced. Good parallel flips are practically impossible with the backhand grip.

1.4.3   SUMMARY

You have now learnt some tactical strategies for playing against certain types of players and know what they can do well, not so well, or not at all.

Don't forget to vary your game though when putting these strategies into practice!

 For example, if you always play to a forehand-dominant player's forehand, sooner or later he will realize and get used to it. He no longer needs to worry about covering his weaker backhand with his forehand but can calmly concentrate on his forehand side.

It is therefore vital that you frequently vary your placement of the ball!

This prevents your opponent from being sure of which shot to expect and allows you to focus on hitting to his weak spots.

Table tennis is not just about hitting the ball over the net, but also placing the ball well.

Careful observation of your opponent's game will reveal where you should or should not hit the ball!

This can already be done in the warm-up stage.

You should also keep an eye on what your opponent is doing during the match itself though!

Whenever you can, adapt your game to your opponent's and make good ball placement choices.

1.5   DRILLS

A   Play a FH topspin from your FH side cross-court to your opponent's wide FH, which he blocks to the center of the table, then play a second FH topspin to his wide BH—he blocks again into your FH side and you play a FH topspin into his elbow—after that play freely!

After 6-8 minutes you can swap over!

In this drill, you should learn how to place your topspin balls precisely. The last topspin to the elbow should be either a killer or a preparation for an offensive final stroke.

Your partner can practice covering the wide FH and BH sides. Reduce running in between shots to a minimum. If the ball comes to the wide FH, take a short cut and take a step with your right leg almost under the table—i.e. forwards and to the right!

The same is true for balls that come very wide on your BH side, in which case you should take a step left and forwards, so that your left leg moves around the table!

B   Play a BH topspin from the BH side—your partner always returns to your BH side with a block shot, first pull cross-court, then parallel and then to the elbow, after that play freely!

Swap roles after 6-8 minutes!

C   Play a short serve freely anywhere in the net area, your partner plays long (baseline area) to your elbow or to your FH side (push or flip), you play a FH topspin to his elbow—he plays a free block return and you play a decisive topspin or smash into one of the two corners—after that play freely!

After about 6-8 minutes, swap roles!

This drill practices a match-specific move. A well-placed topspin to the elbow should set up your offensive final stroke!

That is also why your partner's block is a free shot. He will actually hardly have the chance to play a good return if you have just managed to find his elbow!

Your partner also gets the chance to practice sidestepping these balls with good footwork and returning them under control!

D   Play short or quick and long serves to the elbow—after that play freely!

Swap over after about 6-8 minutes!

Remember that for short serves, the elbow placing point shifts slightly to the FH side!

PACE

02

2   PACE

This chapter deals with the tactical weapon that seems to be becoming more and more important in modern table tennis—pace.

It is a fact that the sport of table tennis has gotten quicker and quicker during recent years. One example of this is the fact that a defensive player no longer stands a chance if he does not also have a good offensive game. Even the introduction of the new, larger 40 mm balls has not been able to reverse this trend, as the slowing down of the game intended by bringing in a larger ball can be compensated for or prevented by choosing a faster blade or thicker rubber.

2.1   FAST OR SLOW?

The purpose of hitting the ball as fast as possible is to leave your opponent no time to react properly.

His position to the ball will be wrong or he will only be able to hold out his racket if he does manage to get to the ball. His shot will therefore not be dangerous for he has had no time to decide how to play the ball, where to place it and how to spin it.

 *So try to hit all your attacking shots as fast as possible!*

However, you must also weigh up the risk of playing a fast ball. Remember that a point won by your opponent making a simple error counts the same as a point won with a killer topspin!

Chapter 8 (Risk Assessment) deals with this topic in greater detail.

So you should only play very fast when you are confident and well-positioned to hit the ball!

Most of the pace can be achieved with smashes or hard topspins, but counter shots and active block balls can be very quick. Even long, aggressive push balls and quick, varied serves can put the opponent under time pressure if they are well-placed.

But even though here we are concerned with pace, we acknowledge that even quite slow balls can pose problems for the opponent.

If an opponent moves back from the table or is already standing back from the table, just play a gentle, slow block or drop shot or a short, flat push ball!

If they are executed well, your opponent will often be unable to reach these balls or will just play an uncontrolled and non-dangerous return!

This is a good tactic to use against defensive and half-distance players. They sometimes have more problems with slow balls than quick ones. The time pressure that quick balls would put them under already exists due to their position a few steps away from the table.

2.2   CHANGES OF PACE

As we now know that both fast and slow balls are dangerous, changing pace is obviously the most effective tactical weapon! Dimitrij Ovtcharov, the German world class player, often confuses his opponents with his changes of pace.

So, don't limit yourself to playing only fast or only slow but vary the speed of your shots!

This stops your opponent from guessing what shot you are going to play next.

You must always force your opponent to play your game.

It is particularly difficult to switch to a fast game if your opponent's game is slow, but it can be done by means of block shots.

While for fast balls you just need to passively hold out your racket at the right time, it is more difficult to return slow balls.

In the first case you can use the pace of your opponent's shots.

In the second case, you yourself must give pace to slow balls by means of increased forearm and wrist action when blocking.

Always play active and passive blocks on the rise (for more on this, see the next chapter 3 "Flight Height"), as that is where you have most control over the ball!

2.3   DRILLS

A   Pace Change Drill

Play FH topspin cross-court to your partner, which he blocks, for about 6-8 minutes. Vary the pace of your topspins, based on your own assessment of the risks involved!

For example, if you think that your position to the ball is not ideal, play a slow, safe topspin!

But if you do feel confident, hit the ball hard! Once you have mastered the drill, your partner can vary his blocks, i.e. by playing active and hard block returns to your slow topspins or even throwing in the odd passive stop block. This enables you to kill two birds with one stone by practicing both blocks and topspins!

B   Maximal Pace Drill

The best way of practicing maximal pace play is with many-balls-training. Hit topspins, smashes or active blocks as fast as possible!

You can see how fast the ball is by its height before it hits the ground. This is also a good way of monitoring your training progress! Have you improved after a few training sessions?

In this drill, you should make sure that you find your own maximal speed, i.e. the speed at which you hit the ball as fast as possible with a low risk of making an error!

FLIGHT HEIGHT

03

3   FLIGHT HEIGHT

Now that you have learned in the previous chapter that it is important to hit the ball as fast as possible in order to leave your opponent no time to play a good return, in this chapter we deal with the issue of flight height.

3.1   GENERAL

The basic rule is to play the ball as flat as possible whatever the stroke!

Basically, all strokes should be played so that the flight height, which is also responsible for the bounce height on the table, is kept as flat as possible. This decrease the risk to your opponent of returning the ball with a hard smash or topspin.

Bear in mind the old, if not entirely serious tactical tip: "play low, win high!"

In order to play as flat as possible, it is important that you observe the different ball hitting points once your opponent's shots have bounced on your side of the table, as shown in the diagram below:

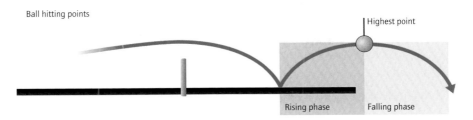

Fig. 10: Ball hitting points

The first phase after the ball bounces is called the **'rising phase.'** Balls in this phase are particularly suited to the following strokes:

- Blocking—against opponent's topspins, smashes or counter shots.
- Countering—against opponent's counter shots.
- Early topspin close to the table—against opponent's topspins.
- Short push balls—against push balls from your opponent.

After a ball has completed the rising flight phase and before it enters the falling phase, there is a brief moment in which the ball reaches its **highest point**. Balls at this point are suited to:

- Smashes—particularly against high chop, blocking and counter shots from your opponent as well as high, mid-length topspins.
- Hard topspin—against block and counter shots from your opponent as well as slightly higher bouncing mid-length and long push balls.
- Flips—against short push balls and all types of short serve.
- Long, aggressive push balls—against push balls from your opponent.

The final flight phase is called the **'falling phase'** and starts as soon as the ball leaves the highest point.

Balls in this flight phase are suited to the following strokes, but should not as a rule be hit below table height:

- Lobs—against opponent's smashes.
- Long, mid-height topspins—against long, flat chops or push balls.
- Backspin defensive strokes—against opponent's topspins and smashes.

NOTE:

It used to be (and sometimes still is) incorrectly assumed that slow topspins have more rotation than fast ones (in this case, topspin), and are therefore more likely to be blocked 'out' more frequently. However, the reason for this is the higher bouncing angle compared to the fast topspin!

In order to give your slow topspins a higher bouncing angle, hit the balls at about table height, as explained above!

As you may already have noticed, there are therefore two exceptions in which you should not hit the ball as flat as possible. We are all familiar with the first, and it is what makes the sport of table tennis so spectacular!

3.2 LOBBING

Anyone who has ever had to play against a good lobbing player knows that it can be very difficult to smash or dropshot very long lobs. They are even more dangerous if topspin is added.

So what amazes us sadly all too rarely on television is not just for show!

If you get into the situation where you need to play lobs, bear in mind the below-mentioned points:

Hit the ball:

- *As high as possible*
- *As long as possible*
- *With as much topspin as possible!*

When is a good time to play a lob?

The answer is: usually after hitting a return that is too high and badly placed, for whatever reason!

If you were just to stay at the table, you would have almost no chance of reaching a hard smash. However, by standing a few meters away from the table, you gain time and are no longer in such a hopeless position.

This brings us to the second exception!

3.3   THE PROBLEM OF TIME

Let's talk about time again.

On the one hand, we know that we play flat balls (that don't travel as far as high ones) in order to leave our opponent no time to hit a good return. On the other hand, we can of course also use this for our own ends.

If, for example, your topspin shot is blocked back to you wide on your forehand side, it will be an effort for you to run to it and you will not be in a good position to hit the ball, so just play a long, soft, mid-height topspin return!

This enables you to gain time in order to get into a good position for the next shot. If you hit the ball too hard, you run the risk that the ball will be returned to the opposite corner and you will not be able to reach it!

3.4 PLAYING AGAINST DEFENSE

One final area in which the flight height is particularly important is when playing against defense.

Defensive players often have trouble returning a slow, mid-height topspin with a flat backspin!

*These can also be **mid-length** if the defensive player is standing (too) far away from the table! Now you know a good tactical strategy for setting up a hard smash or topspin!*

Werner Schlager was able to use just this tactic in 2003 to win the World Championships final against the hitherto unbeaten South Korean defensive player Joo Se Hyuk.

3.5   DRILLS

A   Play topspins to your partner's blocks for about 6-8 minutes. Vary the height of the ball, sometimes soft, slow and high, but long—sometimes hard, fast and flat. Watch your partner's blocks! Is a soft ball a good way of setting up your final shot?

B   Play lobs! Your partner smashes. Try to return the ball as high and as long as possible and with spin. Watch your partner. Does he have trouble returning balls that you hit well?

After 6-8 minutes, swap roles.

C   Serve training: for 15-30 minutes, play any serve you want. You don't need a partner for this. Make sure you hit the ball as late and therefore as low as possible. Check whether it crosses the net flat or too high.

SPIN

04

4   *SPIN*

In this chapter, we explore the phenomenon of spin in a little more detail.

If you know what happens to the ball when it hits the racket, which trajectory it follows and understand how it bounces from the table, then you also need have no fear of older, more experienced players who (try to) confuse you with their curve balls!

There is an answer to everything!

Of course, in our sport, it is much more difficult to handle spin than in other racket sports like tennis or badminton. The vast range of materials with their different effects further complicate things for table tennis players. That is why it is important to be able to spot the rotation that your opponent gives the ball.

At the end of this chapter, we will show you how different kinds of rubbers affect rotation.

But first the big question, how exactly is spin produced?

4.1   PRODUCING SPIN

There are basically two ways of hitting the ball with the racket:

- Flat
- Stroking, or slicing the ball

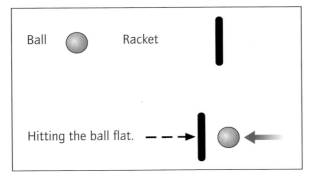

Fig. 11

If you hit the ball flat right in the middle, it leaves your racket with almost no rotation.

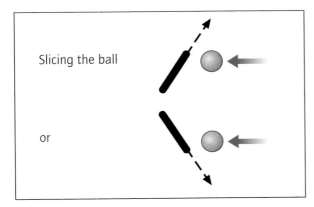

Fig. 12

By slicing it slightly, you give it rotation.

By slicing it from top to bottom, you rotate the ball backwards, which is better known as backspin.

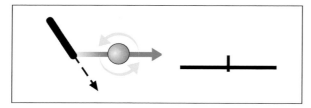

Fig. 13:
Backwards rotation/backspin

The ball turns backwards (around its own axis) as it travels through the air.

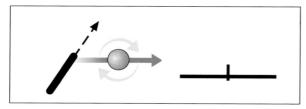

Fig. 14:
Forwards rotation/topspin

By slicing it from bottom to top, you rotate it forwards, otherwise known as topspin. The ball turns forwards as it travels through the air.

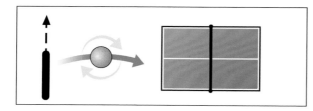

Fig. 15:
Side spin to the right

By slicing it from right to left, you give it sidespin. The ball turns to the right as it travels through the air.

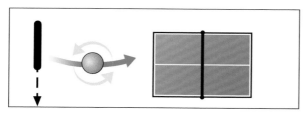

Fig. 16:
Side spin to the left

If you slice it from left to right, you also give it sidespin but this time to the left.

You can, of course, combine backspin and topspin with sidespin, in which case you must slice the ball both sideways and from bottom to top to produce side-topspin, or sideways and from top to bottom to produce side-backspin.

Let's finish with two more comments on spin production:

You can give the ball more spin:

- *By just slicing it gently!*
  The more gently you hit the ball, the more spin you give it!

- *By hitting the ball faster!*
  Slow topspins have less spin than fast ones!

So now you know how rotation or spin is produced. Below we help you to identify what kind of spin your opponent has given the ball.

4.2   IDENTIFYING SPIN

You can only react appropriately to the incoming ball if you know what kind of spin your opponent has given it.

Close observation of how your opponent hits the ball and its resulting trajectory is essential, for it can be hard to get it right, e.g. in the case of serve feints.

4.2.1   BACKSPIN

Backspin is not only used in serves, but also in defensive chops or push balls. We will now expand on the above illustrations.

The question is: how does the ball bounce off a racket if you just hold it out?

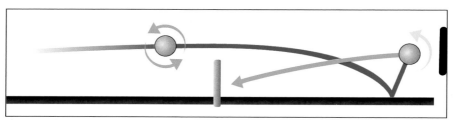

Fig. 17: Holding out the racket straight to hit a ball with backspin.

If you just hold out your racket to a ball with backspin, the backspin will make the ball hit the net.

There are three ways to stop this happening:

Return with a push ball, i.e. slice the ball downwards, which neutralizes the backspin and effectively gives the ball new backspin by reversing the spin direction.

Return with a topspin, i.e. pull the ball upwards, thereby preserving the same direction of rotation and giving the ball topspin.

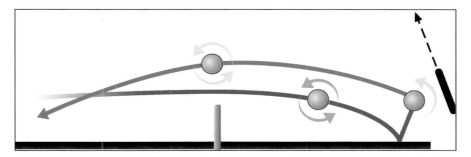

Fig. 18: Preserving spin direction (perspective 1)

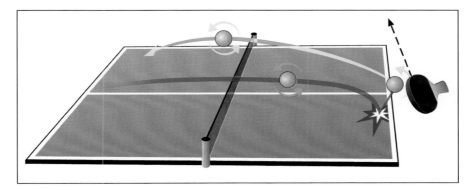

Fig. 19: Preserving spin direction (perspective 2)

Use your opponent's spin and flip the ball (if the ball is short) or smash it (if the ball is long), hitting the ball at its highest point and—as strange as it may sound—with a flat racket! (See photos 14 and 15).

Make sure that you hit the ball slightly beyond your target (baseline of the table), as it were. Your ball will not go out though, but drop onto the table.

This is because by hitting with a flat racket you preserve the existing spin but as the flight direction has changed, the ball now has forwards rotation, i.e. topspin, and it is this topspin that ensures that the ball drops at the right time.

Photo 14

Photo 15

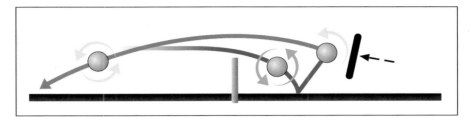

Fig. 20: Trajectory of a flipped ball with backspin (perspective 1)

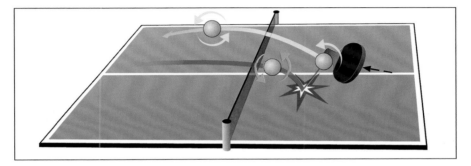

Fig. 21: Trajectory of a flipped ball with backspin (perspective 2)

Smashing a ball with backspin—particularly if the ball is flat—is relatively difficult and is mainly practiced by attacking players with short-pips-out surfaces and by attacking defensive players, such as e.g. the two-time German women's champion Jing Tian-Zörner.

It is relatively easy to learn how to flip short balls with heavy backspin.

4.2.2 TOPSPIN

Topspin is used in the topspin stroke, as its name suggests, but also more and more often in the kick serve.

If you hold your racket out to hit a ball with topspin, depending on the strength of the spin, it will land 'out' on the other side of the net.

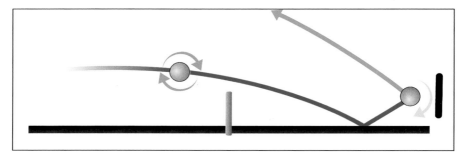

Fig. 22: What happens when you just hold out your racket to hit a ball with topspin.

There are two possible options:

Block the ball with a closed racket blade, hitting it flat. The more spin the ball has, the more you must close the racket blade!

Respond with a topspin, i.e. slice the ball upwards with an extremely closed racket blade. The hitting direction must be more forwards than upwards as otherwise your topspin ball will fly off the table. The spin direction is reversed, but the ball still contains topspin!

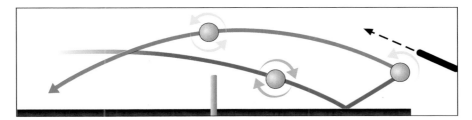

Fig. 23: Reversing the spin direction (perspective 1)

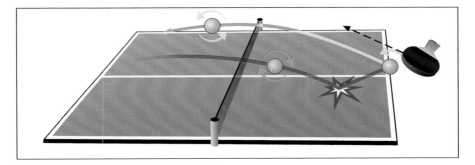

Fig. 24: Reversing the spin direction (perspective 2)

When the spin direction is reversed, the type of spin is preserved (e.g. topspin on topspin → the incoming ball has topspin → your ball also has topspin—see figs 23 and 24).

If the spin direction stays the same, the type of spin changes and the spin is increased (e.g. topspin on backspin → the ball arrives with heavy backspin and leaves your racket with even more topspin—see figs 18 and 19).

4.2.3 SIDESPIN

The strokes in which heavy sidespin can cause particular problems are the serve and the sidespin.

The question once more is:

How does the ball leave the racket if you just hold it out straight?

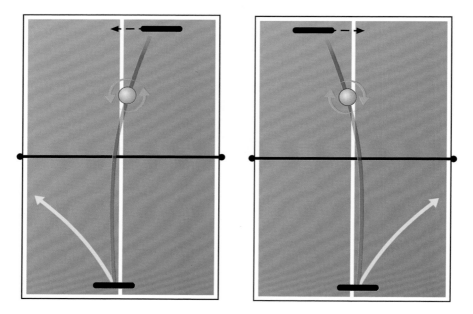

Fig. 25: Racket held out straight with left spin.   Fig. 26: Racket held out straight with right spin.

In plain English: if you just stick out your racket to hit a ball with heavy sidespin, it will land to the side of the table. The direction of movement of your opponent's racket determines whether it goes out to the left or right of the table.

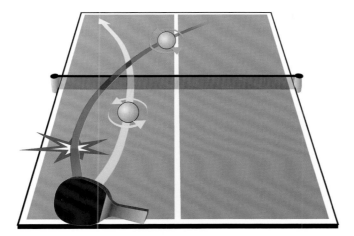

Fig. 27: Return of serve with left spin (perspective 1)

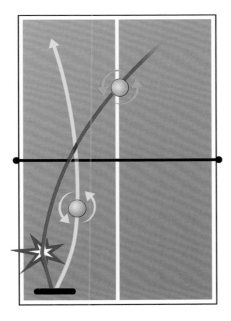

Therefore, it isn't so important to know whether the ball has left or right spin, but to know the direction of rotation (i.e. the direction of movement of your opponent's racket).

Fig. 28:
Return of serve with left spin (perspective 2)

Now you know this, you can return a serve with heavy sidespin by simply hitting it soft forwards in the direction of spin! When executed correctly, this preserves or even increases your opponent's spin!

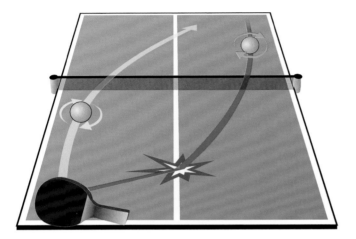

Fig. 29: Return of serve with right spin (perspective 1)

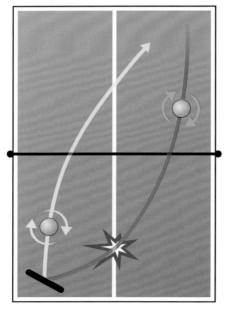

Fig. 30:
Return of serve with right spin (perspective 2)

Incidentally, if you are unable to accurately identify your opponent's movement, just hit the ball down the center line! Try to touch the ball with your racket just for a very short moment!

This reduces the effect of the spin on your return. If you still have trouble with it, wait slightly longer before going to hit the ball; the strength of the slice will gradually diminish. Keep calm! You have more time than you think!

To finish with, here are a few key tips for identifying spin:

- The more quietly your opponent hits the ball, the more spin he has given it! So note how loudly your opponent hits the ball!
- You can also try to work out how fast the ball is spinning or how much slice it has by watching the stamp on the ball, e.g. when receiving serve!
- The faster the ball was pulled or given backspin, the more rotation it is given! So keep an eye on the speed of movement of your opponent's racket!
- If two topspins are hit with the same speed, the one with the most curved trajectory has the most spin! This comparison also applies to sidespins, so observe the flight curve of your opponent's balls closely!

- The further the ball travels, the less spin it has! The spin decreases as the ball flies, so the longer you wait to play your return, the less spin the incoming ball will have! Delay your return slightly if you cannot cope with a sliced serve!

4.3   DRILLS

Before you start with the following drills for chops, topspins, blocks and flips, just take a brief look at the theoretical background of each stroke! Then you can finally start practicing!

4.3.1   CHOP DRILLS

A   Stand in an empty part of the sports hall and mark out two lines 2 and 4 meters away (either use existing lines or mark them with skipping rope or chalk, etc.).

Now hit the ball beyond the markings, with backspin!

If the ball doesn't have enough backspin, it will not bounce once it hits the ground. If it has a lot of backspin, it will even roll backwards. The further back it rolls, the more backspin it has!

B   Now you have the first feel for how to produce backspin, you can go to the table with a partner or your coach.

Play short push balls to him covering the whole table. Try to vary the amount of backspin you give the ball. Your partner should just react to your shots and let you know how successful your attempts were. Swap roles after about 5 minutes.

4.3.2   TOPSPIN AND BLOCK DRILLS

A   Play FH topspins cross-court from your FH side. Your partner plays block returns.

Alternate between playing two topspins in which you spin the ball as gently as possible and then two topspins in which you hit the ball with a quite flat racket. When blocking, your partner must concentrate on the difference between the spins and adapt his racket blade accordingly. Swap roles after 5-8 minutes!

In this drill, your partner does not necessarily have to tell you how successful your spin was. You can see this for yourself in his blocks or attempted blocks. If you just spin the ball lightly, the block will tend either to go out or to be returned relatively high.

If you hit the ball with a quite flat racket while making your hitting action look as unvarying as possible, your partner will block the ball into the net every so often (topspin feint).

This drill can of course also be performed with BH topspin!

B   You play a short backspin serve freely over the whole table.

Your partner plays a long push ball to your forehand.

You open with a cross-court FH topspin with heavy spin.

He hits a block return to your forehand.

You keep on hitting FH topspin returns to your partner's cross-court blocks.

Be aware of the difference between returning a backspin with topspin and a block with topspin! Vary the amount of spin when hitting a topspin return to the blocks.

Swap over after about 6-8 minutes!

This drill can of course also be played with backhands, or instead of cross-court, you can also hit parallel!

4.3.3   FLIP DRILLS

A   Serve short with backspin all over the table!

Your partner plays short push balls to your forehand.

Flip freely all over the table!

Then play freely!

Swap roles after 6-8 minutes!

Practice backhand flips also!

B   It doesn't matter who serves, just play short push balls all over the table. If one player thinks the ball is in the right position he should flip it. After that, play freely! Look for the right ball for the killer flip, or at least the flip that will help you win the point!

The drill should last about 8 minutes!

4.4   SPECIAL KINDS OF RUBBERS

All comments on spin in this chapter only concern the game with normal pips-in rubbers and with restrictions also on short pips-out rubbers. However, a variety of other rubber types exists, which is why we have decided to point out the differences in the game against players using special kinds of rubbers compared to ones who use normal rubbers.

This will, of course, give players who themselves use special kinds of rubbers valuable information for their own game, too.

But first a couple of questions: what are special kinds of rubbers? And what are normal ones?

Our answers employ the usual table tennis jargon. It is quite simple:

Normal describes all rubbers that are not antispin (antis) or pips-out (pips). These are called special kinds of rubbers. Players with special rubbers are therefore those who play with pips or antis on one or both sides of the racket.

Let us take a closer look at the wide range of possible surfaces.

There are flat pips-in rubbers, antis and short, mid-length and long pips. There are rubbers with thick or thin underlying sponge layers (sponge) and also ones without sponge. There are rubbers with soft sponge and those with hard sponge. There are slow rubbers and fast ones and there are rubbers with good grip and not such good grip.

In case you are now completely confused, here are a few rules that apply to all rubber types:

- The thicker the sponge, the faster the rubber!
- The softer the sponge, the better the feel for the ball!
  When the ball hits the racket, it stays on the racket for longer before leaving it. Although only a matter of a fraction of a second, you will notice that it gives you better control of the ball.

- The more grip the surface has, the more spin it can give!
  Beware of a double effect though: although you can produce more spin, you are more likely to make a mistake when hitting your opponent's spinned return!

- The longer the pips, the greater their so-called 'disruptive effect'.
- The greater the disruptive effect, the harder it is to control the rubber!
  Some players with long pips don't always know where their balls are going!

*Here is another tip: don't play with thick and therefore fast rubbers too early on! Remember that even when learning the basic strokes (e.g. topspin, counters, etc.) it is important to have a slightly slower racket that forgives small technical errors and most importantly gives you a **feel for the stroke**! You should also bear this in mind when choosing your blade.*

It is advisable to follow the advice of a specialist retailer. He needs to know as much information as possible about you and your game. Your coach can of course also do this job.

4.4.1 PIPS-IN RUBBERS

What does this mean?

If you look at this type of rubber, you can see that it is effectively composed of two parts. The bottom part is the sponge onto which the top layer is stuck, and if you look closely, you will see that this is none other than a pips-out rubber stuck on back to front, i.e. with the pips facing inside.

Incidentally, the rubbers you are familiar with are not produced and sold everywhere. In the table tennis super-power China for example, until recently one could only buy sponges and top layers separately. Perhaps the reason for this and for the term 'pips-in' is the fact that previously people only played with 'pips out' surfaces and only later started to stick sponge under the top layer in order to speed up their game.

Pips-in surfaces have a non-slip top layer, which makes it easier to produce heavy spin. There are also pips-in surfaces which are different though.

4.4.1.1   ANTIS

These rubbers are used rarely and usually in the lower levels. Their top layers only have very little grip and the sponge is usually very slow.

How should one play against a player who uses antis?

- *The most important thing to remember is that you yourself can determine the spin your opponent uses for his next shot!*
- *Once you have assimilated this fact, you will no longer have trouble playing opponents who use antis!*
- *As your opponent is almost unable to produce spin due to the smooth top layer of the anti, the ball is always returned to you with exactly the opposite spin that you gave your last shot!*

That means that:

If you push the ball with a slight backspin, the opponent's return may also be a push ball, with slight topspin. You can pull it hard forward or even smash it!

If you get involved in a counter rally, you should bear in mind that the ball comes towards you comparatively slowly and does not, as otherwise usual in counter shots, have a little topspin but a little backspin. Open your racket blade a little more than normal and move a little closer to the ball due to its slow pace!

If you play a topspin with heavy spin, the return shot that follows (this is usually a backspin defensive shot or a block) will have heavy backspin. Push the next ball or open your racket blade and pull the ball upwards if you want to play another topspin shot!

The only exception in which you do not get back from your opponent the opposite of your rotation is a ball with heavy backspin, which is returned with just a slight topspin!

4.4.2 PIPS-OUT RUBBERS

As you have already learned in this chapter, there are three different kinds of pips-out top layers: short, mid-length and long pips.

Let's start by looking at short pips.

4.4.2.1 SHORT PIPS

Pips are described as short if they are shorter than 1mm. They used to be used exclusively by uncompromising, offensive penhold grip players, who tried to dictate rallies with hard shots. Short pips are now often used on a combined racket, which means special kind of rubber on the BH side and a normal one on the other.

But there are defensive players who also play with short pips. The reason for all of this is revealed below.

Short pips are less 'sticky' than pips-in rubbers as there is a lot of space between the pips on their top layer. This gives balls played with short pips a flatter trajectory, particularly in topspin shots.

Short pips also make one less susceptible to spin. With a fast sponge underneath, this top layer is extremely suitable for fast block shots and powerful final shots. The lack of sponge or very thin sponge allows for a very good feel for the ball and optimal ball control.

The reason why some elite defensive players use short pips is the possibility of changing spin. For example, a topspin can sometimes be given heavy backspin, sometimes just a little backspin, which is very unsettling for the opponent.

This is impossible with long pips, as you will see in section 4.4.2.2.

How to play against short pips:

If your opponent pushes a ball with short pips, the ball usually has less backspin that you are used to from a normal kind of rubber!

However, it is also possible to produce heavy backspin with short pips!

You just need to watch the top Chinese players who manage to play very heavily spinned serves with their penhold grips and short pips. Jörg Roßkopf was on the receiving end of this in the 1996 Olympics in Atlanta where he lost against Liu Guoliang in the half final who became later Gold Medal Winner in this competition.

The 'stickiness' of short pips-out top layers can vary.

So if you notice that you often hit the ball out when your opponent pushes a ball, just close your racket blade more and pull the ball slightly further forwards (than upwards)!

If your opponent with short pips blocks your topspin, hit the ball earlier! This is important as otherwise it will go into the net. If you reach the ball too late, pull it up with a slightly wider open racket blade!

If you have to return a block or counter shot from short pips, you should also open your racket blade slightly! The follow through can also finish higher to back up the action!

4.4.2.2   LONG PIPS

Pips longer than 1.5 mm are referred to as long pips. Long pips without sponge give a better feedback (more control) than those with sponge backing, but this makes them somewhat slower. Both have a great disruptive effect, which makes a game against long pips impossible to read for many players.

However, once you have understood how long pips work, it is really not so hard!

 *Long pips can only produce limited spin!*

Consequently:

If you play without spin, even if your opponent uses a strong forearm and wrist action, the ball is returned with little spin, or usually with no spin at all!

If you play a topspin and your opponent blocks with his long pips or defends the ball, the pips fold and give the ball **backspin**.

You can either play safe and push these shots or pull them with topspin but with a more open racket blade and more upwards than usual.

 Remember: The more spin your topspin has, the more backspin comes back to you!

If you push and your opponent pushes back with long pips, the ball has **topspin**! You must therefore pull forward (topspin) or can smash it.

NOTE:

On no account make the common error of trying to push the ball back with an open racket blade. This stroke always bounces too high due to the topspin on the incoming ball and can then be attacked very easily by your opponent.

The characteristics of long pips described above mean that there are a few very good ways of playing against long pips:

 Serve to long pips short or long with backspin (not sidespin!), or with no spin at all and then follow up with a killer topspin! If this is returned, you can push again into the long pips and the whole thing starts all over again!

Because of the predictability of long pips, some defensive players, are changing to play with short pips instead or flip the racket to play with the normal rubber. In this way they are able to produce their own spin.

We would like to end by explaining how curved or even swerving balls are played with long pips.

If the ball is hit with long pips and only a very slightly closed (e.g. block) or very slightly open racket blade (e.g. aggressive push), the pips don't fold. The same also applies for shots in which the ball is hit with a flat racket, in which case they are squashed, i.e. pushed or squeezed together instead of folding.

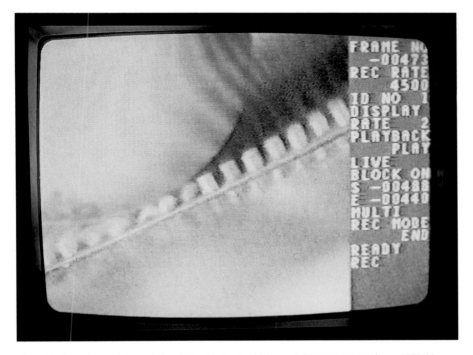

Photo 16: How pips are deformed when hitting the ball at high speed. (BUTTERFLY Catalogue 1998-99, English edition, page 5).

How much the pips are squashed depends on the power of the incoming ball and the hitting power of the player using the long pips. Of course, it also depends on the amount of spin of the incoming ball and the position of the racket blade when it hits the ball.

The effect on the ball of all of the above-mentioned factors explains the great variety of these shots.

Are you still with us or have you switched off already?

If you cannot cope with these swerving balls, try to hit them relatively late when they have less spin!

This also gives you more time to observe and identify the spin of the ball.

4.4.2.3   MID-LENGTH PIPS

Pips between 1 and 1.5 cm are called mid-length pips. Their disruptive effect is weaker, but this gives them greater stability than long pips. Mid-length pips are often used for backhands in order to return the ball under control.

Here are some final comments to players who play with special kinds of rubbers on one side of the racket and a normal rubber on the other side.

Get your opponent to show you his racket if you suspect that he is using special kinds of rubbers!

Remember: e.g. black rubber = long pips!

In a game, check if your opponent flips his racket, for example, he doesn't always play with the long pips on the backhand side, but sometimes on the forehand side!

If he does flip, try to speed up the game so that he doesn't have time to do it!

SERVICE TACTICS

05

5.1 SERVICE FEINTS

5.2 TIPS FOR SERVICE TRAINING

5 SERVICE TACTICS

In modern table tennis, the serve is very important as it is the only stroke which does not involve a reaction to a previous shot from your opponent, which means that it can be played without any time pressure.

What do we want to achieve with a good serve?

The aim of a good serve is to:

- (At best) to score the point directly.
- Start the rally well, i.e. the serve should prepare a good first ball or ensure that we can exploit our strengths.
- Play deliberately to our opponent's weaknesses or at least stop him from exploiting his strengths.

In order to achieve these objectives, before every serve you should bear the following in mind:

Where do I want to place my serve?

You should place long serves on your own side of the table as near to the baseline area and as flat as possible! This is the only way to be able to hit equally long, flat and hard, irrespective of which type of spin you have decided to use.

For short or mid-length serves, when the opponent can only see very late whether the ball would bounce a second time if it wasn't hit, you should place the ball about 30-50 centimeters in front of the net on your side of the table.

Make up your mind, particularly for crosscourt serves, whether it is a good idea to play the serve more from your backhand or forehand side—think about the scattering angle!

Which typical strengths or weaknesses stand out in your opponent's game and what are they? Notice the differences between forehand and backhand dominant players.

How fast should my serve be?

Play long serves as fast as possible, but without losing control.

Short and mid-length serves must be relatively slow, as otherwise they will be too long.

How high should my serves be?

Hit all serves the same, irrespective of which placing, pace or spin you have chosen, i.e. as low as possible over the net!

Which type of spin should I give my serve?

A serve can be sliced in all different ways, but watch your opponent constantly to see which type of spin he finds hardest to deal with—keep an eye on his racket grip, too!

When serving, vary both the direction and amount of spin! You can use the service feints described in the following section.

It is basically true that:

Your serves must be appropriate for your type of game, i.e. help you to play your own game!

A positive example of this is provided by the Pole Andrej Grubba, who sadly died before his time. During the game he always threw in the odd very short, flat and almost sliceless serves in the center of the opponent's side of the table. However, he rarely won direct points with them, although these serves did present the opponent with a different problem: a dangerous return was very hard to play as these nonspun serves can easily be hit out with a hard flip or an aggressive, long push ball, or only a relatively harmless return made the rest of the rally easier for Grubba to win. All he had to do was attack these harmless returns with his forehand or backhand, which was an ideal opening move as he was an excellent half-distance player.

So test your serve to see if you can score points directly with it or start something with the possible returns from your opponent!

The best plan is to have as varied a service game as possible, i.e. change placing, spin and pace as much as possible so that your opponent doesn't know what kind of serve to expect!

However, exactly the opposite can be observed among young up-and-coming players, as they always play the same serve **without thinking**.

Also think of making the second service in your group of two serves different to the first, e.g. don't always start or finish with the same serve!

We suggest you serve predominantly short or mid-length serves and throw in the odd long and fast serves.

Note which serves give your opponent the most trouble and save them for important match situations or for the end of the match!

This prevents your opponent from finding out during the match how to deal with these serves and gives you an ace up your sleeve for the end of the match!

The effectiveness of your serve is not only determined by the spin, placing and pace, but is also critically dependent on whether or not you can make it difficult or even impossible for your opponent to spot the spin and placing of the coming shot. This can be done by means of service feints.

5.1 SERVICE FEINTS

Below we describe the service feints with which you can give the ball completely different types of spin, using what appears to be the same service action.

Use these pointers in the future for your own serves but when returning serve, watch your opponent closely to make sure that he isn't using them too!

5.1.1 FEINTS WITH OR WITHOUT SPIN

In the with/without spin feint, by changing the angle of the racket when the ball is hit or the amount of wrist action (or a combination of the two), you can alternate between playing a serve with and without or with very little spin with an otherwise identical service action.

Some servers also stamp one foot when hitting the ball to stop their opponent from working out how much spin the serve has by listening to the noise of the racket hitting the ball.

Two other feints in which can vary the spin by the time ball hitting point with otherwise identical actions are serves that are executed according to the windscreen wiper principle and the reverse principle.

5.1.2   THE 'WINDSCREEN WIPER' PRINCIPLE

The main hitting direction is arc-shaped in the windscreen wiper principle.

The arc is open at the top for a typical high-thrown forehand serve (with right spin) from the backhand side and for a backhand serve with left spin.

If you hit the ball before the mid-point of the arc, i.e. in the first phase of the movement, you give it side-backspin!

Photo 17: If you hit it at the mid-point, i.e. in this backhand serve at the lowest point of the arc, you give the ball sidespin!

Photo 18: If you hit the ball after the mid-point, i.e. in the last phase of the movement, you give the ball side-topspin!

5.1.3 THE REVERSAL PRINCIPLE

Photos 19 and 20: In forehand serves played according to the reverse principle, you can change the direction of sidespin.

When using the wind-screen wiper principle the ball was given the same direction of sidespin at all three hitting points. When using the reversal principle hitting the ball before the turning point gives it sidespin to the right.

However, if the ball is hit after the turning point, it is given sidespin to the left.

NOTE:

Timo is a lefthander! He therefore produces a left spin when hitting before the turning point (photo 19). Photo 20 shows Timo just after he has hit the ball after the turning point, having given it right spin.

5.2   TIPS FOR SERVICE TRAINING

 *Always try to make service training an integral part of your weekly training program!*

The best servers practice their serves daily!

First practice your serves alone, i.e. without a partner to return them!

Take a number of balls and play serves of your choice for 15-30 minutes!

It is up to you what your serves looks like; don't restrict your creativity!

During a service training session you can either practice several different serves or focus on one particular serve!

Try out new serves!

If you run out of ideas, consult your coach or just watch what other players are doing!

RETURN TACTICS

06

6   RETURN TACTICS

Now that you have learned how to use your serves to your best advantage, we want to give you some tips on how to disarm an opponent's serve. In doing so we will focus on returns after short serves and those that bounce midway on your half of the table with sidespin (combined with backspin or topspin).

What is special about these returns is that the sidespin is reversed and the returns to the opposing serves can be made particularly dangerous with major sidespin components.

NOTE:

The first European player to successfully use this return technique was Jan-Ove Waldner, who learned it by watching the Penholder players during his training in China.

In order to choose the right return technique it is important to recognize whether the ball spins left or right when it bounces on your half of the table.

Why Is That So Important?

It is important because the return must spin in the opposite direction, meaning the approaching sidespin must be reversed.

You can see this in the following illustrations.

Push Return Technique with FH and BH for Serves with Sidespin to the Left

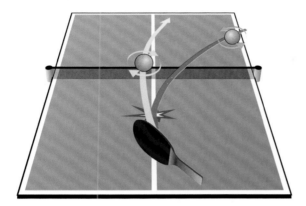

Fig. 31: Angle 1

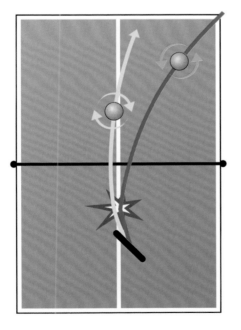

Fig. 32: Angle 2

PLEASE NOTE:

The approaching spin to the left digs into the rubber of the slanted racket as it moves from left rear to right front, turning the opposing left spin into a right spin. The slant of the racket must be such that the incoming serve does not go through to the blade. That is why a good return with lots of spin is always very quiet.

It is the opposite when the incoming ball spins to the right (see figures 33 and 34). Pay attention to the angle of the racket. Now the stroke movement is right rear to left front. The approaching opposing right spin becomes left spin.

Push Return Technique with FH and BH for Serves with Sidespin to the Right

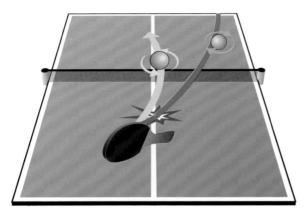

Fig. 33: Angle 1

The ball digging into the rubber causes a kind of catapult effect, especially if the stroke was short and dynamic. The result is that your opponent's sidespin is returned to him (in a reverse direction) with much more spin.

NOTE:

When Jan-Ove Waldner used these techniques against his European opponents they were so unsettled by the returning sidespin that some of them decided to put less spin on their serves against him.

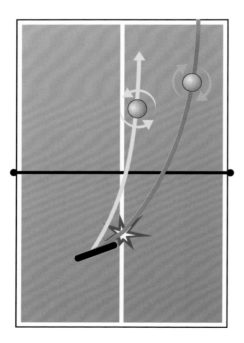

Fig. 34: Angle 2

BH Sidespin (also Called Chiquita or Banana Flick) as a Serve Return over the Table

When watching the serve returns to short- and mid-table sidespin serves (combined with backspin or topspin) of top international players, it is apparent that there are many more backhand returns than forehand returns. Even just a few years ago, players who were particularly forehand dominant used forehand techniques almost exclusively over the entire table.

WHY THIS CHANGE?

When looking at human anatomy, one can see that it is easier to perform backhand strokes over the table because with these techniques the ball is struck in front of the body and the table is less in the way than with forehand techniques, where the ball is to the front and side of the body. This is especially true for returns to mid-table serves.

WHY IS THIS RETURN SPIN TECHNIQUE PLAYED WITH A SIDESPIN (FOR RIGHT-HANDERS WITH SPIN TO THE RIGHT)?

This technique has two major advantages. The first is the backswing motion for this stroke. With a normal backhand topspin over the table in response to the opponent's spin (particularly side- or backspin), the backswing can be very short because the table limits the downward movement. But if the backswing is performed to the side (right) and back over the table, the table is not in the way and the motion can be longer.

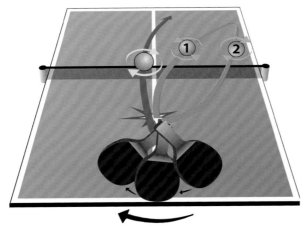

Fig. 35

The second reason is that this return technique can be executed in response to opposing sidespin techniques that pull to the right (see ball 2) as well as to the left (see ball 1). This makes it a dangerous all-purpose weapon against any short- and mid-distance sidespin serves that are returned over the table.

If the opposing serve pulls to the left (from the view of the returning player), the incoming sidespin is taken along and can be intensified with the wrist movement.

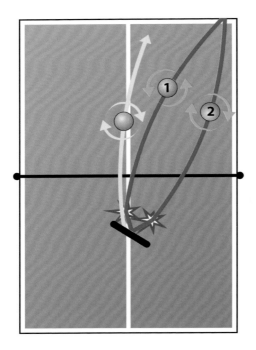

Fig. 36

However, if the opposing serve pulls to the right (from the view of the returning player), the return is executed the same way. In doing so the incoming opposing sidespin is reversed, meaning the opposing spin digs into the rubber and the direction of the sidespin changes from right pull to left pull. The previously described digging in and the wrist movement produce a kind of catapult effect. The incoming sidespin serve is returned with a different sidespin direction (from right pull to left pull). The catapult effect gives the returning ball a stronger rotation (more sidespin) than that of the incoming serve.

NOTE:

The former German men's singles European champion Dimitri Ovtcharov and the young Chinese phenomenon Fan Zhendong are two players who use this technique particularly often. Zhendong was only sixteen years old when he won the German Open in 2013. Like many other top players, they play backhand dominant over the table and forehand dominant behind the table.

Surfing Tip

You can find video footage of these two players as well as many other top players at www.tt-action.de.

DOUBLES

07

7   DOUBLES

It happened more than a quarter century ago, but for many table tennis fans it is the greatest success in German table tennis.

In 1989, Jörg Roßkopf and Steffen Fetzer became men's doubles world champions, and they did it at home at the Westphalia Hall in Dortmund, Germany.

When asked about the secret to their success during an interview for a sports program that same night—in addition to crediting a fantastic crowd that helped them get into a regular playing frenzy—they stated that there was likely no other doubles team in the world as tight as theirs.

Rossi and Speedy were thick as thieves back then and even lived together in a living community.

Does this mean you have to be friends to be successful as doubles?

In this chapter we will take a closer look at this question as well as some others, so we can help you become a good doubles player.

7.1 EVERYTHING IS DIFFERENT

In table tennis, doubles players must alternate hitting the ball. There are exceptions to this rule in disabled sports, which we will not elaborate on at this time.

Doubles partners must work well together, because as a player one never receives the opposing response to their own ball but rather that of their partner's ball. For this reason there is great demand for team players who not only know as much as possible about their opponents, but also know about and take into consideration their partner's strengths and weaknesses.

You don't necessarily have to be friends to be in sync with your doubles partner, but you must respect each other and, most importantly, you must be able to tolerate your partner's mistakes.

When his partner makes a mistake, a good doubles player always looks to himself for potential mistakes: "Was my serve too long? Was my placement to imprecise?"

Furthermore, it requires trust. Doubles players must possess self-confidence as well as confidence in their partner and their teamwork.

At the table you can quickly see whether or not a doubles pair's chemistry is right.

Good doubles pairs move similarly. They both run to the corner to retrieve the ball. They go to the towel together. They talk a lot to each other and have a lot of contact.

The two best singles players do not automatically make the best doubles pair; in fact, a well-functioning doubles team consisting of two weaker singles players can definitely defeat a considerably stronger opponent.

7.1.1 COMMUNICATION MATTERS

Even if as a spectator one has the impression that a pair can communicate wordlessly—blind in a way—a doubles pair should talk to each other a lot because only in doubles is it permissible to do so during a set. This provides an excellent opportunity for coaching each other during a game. And it is not always about tactics. It is also about the partner's mental state. For instance, if he seems anxious, a few words of encouragement can help, or the other player can take charge of the game until the partner is more relaxed and playing more confidently. If he gets too revved up, you can bring him back down and provide the necessary composure and concentration.

In doubles it is often advantageous if one partner is in charge. But the consequences of decisions made—positive or negative—must always be borne by both players.

7.2 CHOOSING A PARTNER— OPPOSITES ATTRACT

This can apply to different types of players. Often a reliable preparer works well with an aggressive scorer. Both player types compliment each other and become a strong unit. That was also the case with the world champion doubles pair, Roßkopf and Fetzner.

But this also applies to so-called handedness. Here the combination of a right-hander and a left-hander is most promising because they move in different areas within the box and therefore don't get in each other's way. In addition most attacking players tend to play forehand dominant, and with a right–left combination both players are able to use their powerful forehand strokes without long running paths.

Moreover, left-handers are particularly valuable in doubles because they have some advantages over right-handers in doubles. Left-handers are able to play their serves and returns from their backhand side of the table like they are accustomed to in singles, while right-handers must play them from the less familiar forehand side. Often they don't know where to put their feet, especially during the serve.

By contrast left-handers can practically stand next to the table not only during the serve but also during the return since in doubles they don't have to worry about balls to their wide forehand—that's when it is their partner's turn. So not only do left-handers have a more favorable position for serves and returns, but with their characteristic positional play they at the same time cede the entire table to their right-handed partner.

Many of the right-left combination advantages also apply to right—right pairs if one player is forehand dominant and his partner is backhand dominant. Here the partner with the stronger backhand is the quasi left-hander of the doubles pair. Of course this also applies in reverse to doubles consisting of two left-handers.

Successful doubles pairings are often those whose players prefer different distances to the table because they rarely impede each other in their running paths.

Here the player closest to the table should have a good passive game while his partner at half-distance, due to his playing system, should play balls with lots of spin (topspin or backspin defense).

7.3   SYSTEM OF PLAY

It always makes sense for two players to use the same playing system when playing together (e.g., an attacking player with an attacking player and a defensive player with a defensive player). But as with every rule, there are exceptions. For instance, a defensive player can also form a successful doubles team with an attacker if both players are very familiar with the strengths and weaknesses of the other's playing system and are able to adapt their own playing style to the associated tactical requirements. For example, it is not very helpful to the defending player if you are really good at flipping opposing serves; he is able to do less with the opposing response than a long, aggressive push with lots of backspin from you.

Remember: In doubles your shot is always preparation for your partner, not yourself!

7.4   TECHNICAL QUALIFICATIONS

In doubles it is particularly important to have good serves and good returns because these often decide the outcome of a rally, whether the own partner is pressured or the opposing double is decisively pressured.

But another, often neglected, aspect must also be taken into account.

In singles the technique is often based on the sequence of individual strokes, meaning that one's own next stroke is already being considered as each technique is executed. So, for example, after a forehand topspin your arm should not swing too far out so you are not caught off-guard by a quick response from your opponent and have time to prepare for your next shot.

Everything is different in doubles. Players have much more time for their shots than they do in singles because it's always the partner's turn next. You could even fall down after the shot or literally take big jumps. Unlike in singles, in doubles the likelihood of still successfully finishing the rally is considerably higher.

7.5   MOVEMENT PATTERNS

Another peculiarity of doubles as compared to singles is that not only do you have to efficiently get to the ball, but that you must also efficiently move away because your partner needs space for his shot. To ensure that happens we suggest four specific movement patterns below. Every doubles pair should think about which movement pattern works best for them. You should at least try them out with your partner and preferably practice them periodically in realistic service–return situations.

PATTERN 1: IN AND OUT

This is the ideal movement pattern for a doubles pair with one right-hander and one left-hander. One player approaches the table from the left rear and then retreats the same way. His partner does the same on the other side. Neither player is in the other's way and they can start their game from the backhand corner like they do in singles.

The *in-and-out movement pattern* can also be used by two right-handers or two left-handers if, as was previously mentioned, one plays forehand dominant and the other backhand dominant.

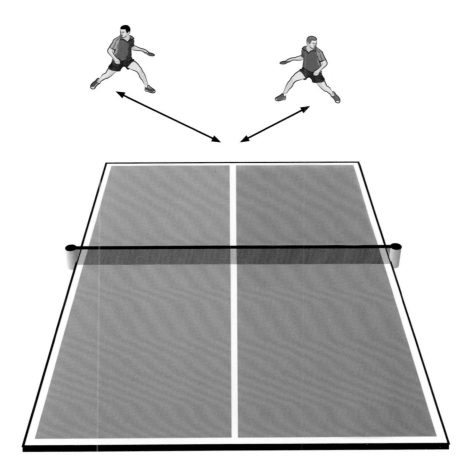

Fig. 37: In-and-out movement pattern

PATTERN 2: CIRCLE

Here the two doubles partners continuously run circles around each other.

This movement pattern works well for pairs playing with the same hand who also prefer the same side, generally forehand. However, implementation requires adjusting to wide paths and warrants good footwork.

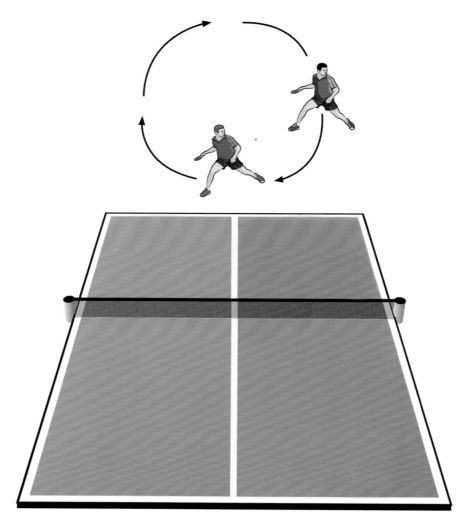

Fig. 38: Circle movement pattern

PATTERN 3: T MOVEMENT

Doubles pairs whose players prefer different distances to the table should choose the T-movement pattern. This can be done, for instance, with a combination of an attacking player who plays close to the table, and a defensive player. This pattern is also best suited for a pairing that consists of an attacking player who feels most comfortable at half-distance, and a blocking player.

The close-range player approaches the table from the side and also retreats to the side, while his partner approaches the table through the center.

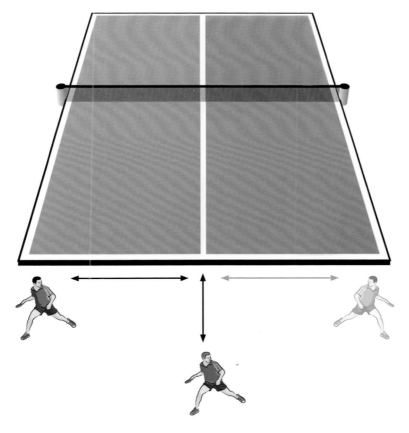

Fig. 39: T-movement pattern

PATTERN 4: 8 MOVEMENT

The 8 movement is a pattern that can be used to return to the starting position on the backhand side after previously having been forced into the wide forehand. In this respect it is not comparable to the other three patterns.

The player who is forced into the wide forehand moves in an arc behind his partner and back to the center of the table where he plays his next shot, and only then does he return to his usual position in the backhand corner. The way back to the backhand side is effectively halved by an in-between shot, and is thereby made much easier.

After that, you simply go back to the preferred movement pattern (in and out, circle or T).

It sounds more complicated than it is. Here, too, the motto is: "Practice makes perfect!"

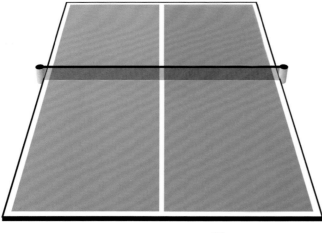

Fig. 40:
8-movement pattern

7.6   TACTICAL TIPS

Doubles players can essentially use the same four tactical means as singles for a successful game. The height of the ball's flight and spin (see chapters 3 and 4) as a tactical means can be used in the same way as in singles, but in doubles there are a few peculiarities with respect to tempo and placement that we will address in more detail below.

7.6.1   THE ART OF DOUBLES IS TO PLAY SLOWER

In chapter 2.1 we recommended that you play all attacking shots as fast as possible to press the opponent for time. In this chapter you learned that the doubles rule of alternating shots makes it much easier to play fast because you have considerably more time to get in the right starting position for your next shot, and you don't have to think about a short swing phase since you don't have to play the next ball yourself.

Is this a contradiction? No, because in doubles a high tempo combined with bad placement can become a disadvantage. We often see these tactical mistakes when a fast diagonal ball is returned as a fast diagonal ball.

7.6.2   PLACEMENT IS EVERYTHING

In doubles, forehand dominant play from the backhand side is of critical importance. Players are able to generate more pressure from the backhand corner. By running around the backhand they make room for their partner, leaving him the entire table for his next ball. And unlike in singles, they do not have to worry about being outplayed in the wide forehand because, as we know, it is the partner's turn before your own next ball. Thus the backhand side is the strong side.

But when you play forehand dominant from the backhand side, the wide forehand (see chapter 1, fig. 2) automatically becomes the weak side or the Achilles' heel.

When a player receives a ball there, not only is he unable to generate as much pressure, but afterwards he is effectively in the wrong corner and has a long way back to his optimal position. If he doesn't get there quickly he must play the subsequent ball with the less forceful backhand.

When playing against forehand-dominant players, in singles (see paragraph 1.4.11) as well as doubles, placement into the wide forehand is a promising tactical tool!

At the same time, when placing your own shots, you also have to make sure that your partner's movement patterns are kept as small as possible.

Here your knowledge on the subject of scattering angles will be helpful (see paragraph 1.2).

In doubles you should play to the corner opposite your partner. In practice this means the following:

In doubles you, and of course your partner, should often play parallel!

Probably the most common placement in doubles is the repeat. This forces the opponents to play two or more consecutive balls from the same position. Even if the opposing double is able to resolve this with good footwork and doesn't get in each other's way, at some point the other corner is open and can be played on.

Afterwards, play the ball with your partner once (or several times) back to where it came from!

If you look closely, you may now see a contradiction here—sometimes one placement tip just doesn't work with the other. For instance, when the wide forehand of the opponent being played on is not in the corner opposite your own partner, the doubles pair must decide if it would be more promising to play for the own partner or against the opponent.

Our tip:

If the opposing double exerts a lot of pressure you should first play on their weak spot to take some pressure out of the game.

But if you happen to be the game-determining pair, we recommend making it as easy as possible for the own partner.

7.7   SERVES: LENGTH MATTERS

In doubles as in singles, the serve is of particular importance.

Half-long serves in particular are very promising here. They are difficult to counter with a short return or to flip, and are also difficult for the opponent to attack.

A serve that is too short can place the opponent far to the outside and is also easier for him to flip.

If the serve is too long, the returning player can immediately and relatively easily attack with a forehand topspin. In doubles, a high tempo also doesn't help with a long serve; due to the rule that the serve must be diagonal the placement options are cut in half.

7.7.1   WITH SPIN OR WITHOUT?

Serve feints without any spin appear to be most effective in doubles (see 5.1.1) because they do not give the opponent the opportunity to use the incoming rotation for the return. The returning player can add little backspin to an empty serve, and will have difficulty flipping hard or playing a short ball.

However, for the server it is easier to place a serve (mid-table) without spin.

7.7.2   SIGN LANGUAGE UNDER THE TABLE

In a successful doubles pair, both partners should always know which actions are options for the opponent. This inevitably means that one partner knows which serve the other intends to play. A quick, long serve is ineffective if it surprises the own partner more than the player on the other side.

Successful doubles partners share this essential information via certain serve signals. The server signals his partner under the table which serve he wants to play with specific hand and finger positions. There are also situations where one partner uses a serve signal to ask for a particular serve.

There are no limits to creativity here. What matters is that both partners know the signals' meaning.

To make sure communication via these serve signals is successful, both partners must know their meaning and must be able to execute the indicated serves more or less reliably. And here, too, the well-trodden motto applies: "Practice makes perfect!"

RISK ASSESSMENT

08

8.1 RISK PHASES

8   RISK ASSESSMENT

One of the most important features of successful players compared to weaker ones is the ability to be realistic about their abilities, so that in matches they usually restrict themselves to what they can do, not what they would like to be able to do.

An example of this is two players who have an equally confident and powerful FH topspin, which is ideally suited for a point-winning final stroke. They are called Steve Strategy and Freddy Freak.

The big difference between them is that Steve Strategy only uses his FH topspin after preparing well for it in the rally by e.g. if his serve is only returned mid-length and too high by his opponent or the opponent only playing a slow, unplaced return block of a slow set-up topspin. In both cases, Steve Strategy now has a good chance of winning the rally (and therefore the point) with his hard FH topspin.

What also characterizes his game and clearly differentiates him from Freddy Freak is that he can also see when he shouldn't use his hard FH topspin, because the risk of making an error is too high. To stick with the two game situations mentioned above, Steve Strategy's opponent could have returned his serve long and flat or have returned his preparation shot with a hard, well-placed block. In both cases, Steve Strategy would have avoided playing his hard FH topspin and continued the rally with a stroke that he was more confident of in this situation.

Freddy Freak, on the other hand, plays his FH final stroke more indiscriminately. Any ball from his opponent that is remotely appropriate is returned with a hard FH topspin, without any prior assessment of the risks or chances of success.

The result of this is that Freddy Freak has a much higher error rate for the same stroke than Steve Strategy.

This comparison may seem too extreme, but it does explain how two players of similar abilities can have such completely different results, not even because one player is technically better than the other, but because Steve Strategy is more able to distinguish between situations where it is appropriate to try to win the rally and those where he should allow the rally to continue instead.

It could also be that Freddy Freak knows that he should prepare his final strokes better in order to play more successfully, but that he lacks the necessary patience and tactical discipline during the match.

8.1   RISK PHASES

The scales illustrated overleaf give you an overview of the five possible risk phases that can exist during a rally.

The further to the bottom right the scales tip (when the traffic lights are green), the greater the chance of winning the rally. However, don't forget that a rally not only usually develops in one direction (serve, preparation shot, final shot), but that often—particularly in the case of longer topspin rallies—the chances for winning the point can vary greatly within the rally.

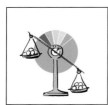

Phase 2   You have put your opponent under so much pressure that you have a good chance of winning the point.

Example: Your opponent has to play lobs.

Phase 1   You take the initiative by playing a preparation shot during the rally and force your opponent into a more passive role.

Example: Your opponent can only play a poor service return.

Phase 0   The rally is at a stalemate. Neither you nor your opponent have an advantage or disadvantage in this phase.

Example: You and your opponent are playing a BH counter-rally.

Phase -1 Your opponent takes the initiative by playing a preparation shot during the rally, thereby forcing you into a more passive role.

Example: Your opponent places you under pressure with an aggressive push ball to your backhand and you are no longer able to respond with a well-placed push ball.

Phase -2 Your opponent has put you under so much pressure that he has a very good chance of winning the point.

Example: You have to play lobs.

How can I use this to benefit my own game?

In practice, it is quite common to see a player who find himself e.g. in phase -2 trying to respond with a smash in order to bring himself into stage 2. If this works, he has a very good chance of winning the rally. However, in most cases, he will not be able to return the ball back onto the table. In this example, the player tries to get from phase -2 to phase 2 in just one stroke, here a counter smash, thus skipping three phases (phases -1, 0 and 1). This may seem very extreme to you, but just think about how many rallies you lose unnecessarily because your block return of your opponent's topspin is too hard and too uncontrolled. It is far better to aim for the next phase up or (with a greater risk) skipping just one phase.

AN EXAMPLE:

You are involved in a BH-counter-rally with an opponent and neither of you has a decisive advantage (phase 0). In order to gain an advantage yourself, you now play a well-placed (but at a pace that you can still control), BH counter deep into your opponent's forehand, in an attempt to force your opponent away from the table and to put him into a passive position (phase 1). If this works, you can then try to out your opponent under further pressure until he either makes an error or you have put him under so much pressure (e.g. with a final offensive shot) that he can no longer get to the ball. However, if in the same situation (BH counter rally/phase 0) you try to skip a phase with a very hard, parallel counter ball, you are a lot closer to winning the point but also to making a mistake yourself.

Which brings us back to the start of the chapter.

This is why it is important that you learn to evaluate your own capabilities as objectively as possible in order to avoid taking unnecessary risks.

NOTE:

Vladimir Samsonov is definitely a world-class player who is an optimal exponent of the above-mentioned way of winning a point without taking unnecessary risks. Like a chess player, he often puts his opponent in an increasingly worse position stroke by stroke, while improving his own, until the rally has been decided in his favor. It is not for nothing that some experts say that table tennis is like chess, but played at 180 km/h.

EPILOGUE

09

9 EPILOGUE

We hope that you have understood everything and learnt many new things.

Now it's up to you to put this theory into practice.

For even if you now know a lot (more) about the game of table tennis, you are still a long way from being able to put it into practice in a match straight away.

Remember, practice makes perfect!

Only if you have experienced certain situations a hundred times in training will you also be able to master them under pressure in a match! This is one reason why it is also so important to play match-like simulation drills in training, not just play games!

If you follow this advice, your expanded knowledge will definitely soon also be visible on the table! You just need to be patient! If anything is still unclear, ask your coach for help. We hope that this book will also have encouraged you to talk and communicate more with your fellow players and coaches, etc., as the more you know about the game, the more interesting and exciting it is!

By the way, at the end of the next chapter there is a questionnaire that acts as a kind of small test, which should show you how much you have learned about table tennis. The answers appear at the end.

So sound out your coach to see how much he knows about tactics! Maybe he can even learn something from you!

THE OFFICIAL RULES

10 THE OFFICIAL RULES

You've seen it many times: animated discussions between parents and coaches as to whether the serve just played was in or out, or fights about who should receive service from whom in the second set of the doubles. The internationally valid Official Table Tennis Rules for the 2016/17 season contained in this chapter will help to settle such disagreements.

Even if you don't understand everything straight away (it usually sounds much more complicated than it really is), at least you now have an answer in black and white that you can show your opponent in the case of doubt and dispute!

This chapter is not only intended for consultation in the case of differences of opinion though; we also take a closer look at two rules that relate to tactical decisions. The first concerns Rule 13 of part A of the Official Rules.

10.1   THE ORDER OF SERVING, RECEIVING AND ENDS

If you have understood this rule, you can use it to your tactical advantage! It goes as follows:

If before the game you win the lot, you can choose either to serve or receive serve first or to start at a particular end!

If you decide to receive serve first (your opponent must serve, but can decide which end to choose), although you may be at a disadvantage at the start of the first set because your opponent can serve first, at the end of the first, third and should the occasion arise, the fifth or seventh (and deciding) set in the case of close matches (e.g. 9:9, 8:10, 10:8) it is your serve when in the last phase the expedite system comes into play.

AS A RESULT:

You always have one more possibility of deciding the game at the end of a set with your own serve than your opponent does, irrespective of whether you are playing the best of three or four sets.

If you have problems receiving serve, if you win the right to choose service you should choose to serve so you don't fall behind too quickly (e.g. 1:5).

If you think you can cope well with the serves or are yourself a good server, choose to receive serve first so that you can, for example use your strong serve to bring the score to 3:1 in a 1:1 situation!

You should only choose a specific end if there is a significant difference in playing conditions between the two ends!

For example, the sun in your eyes, a white background or irritating noise.

If there is something that could distract you—choose the best side first!

If matches end with a score of 3:0 or in the best of four sets, 4:1, you then always have the advantage of playing one more time at the better end.

Remember though that if you choose ends you lose the chance to choose to serve or receive!

The second rule that we consider to be worth highlighting from a tactical point of view is Rule 15.

10.2 THE EXPEDITE SYSTEM

The Expedite System explains which rules change if a set lasts longer than 10 minutes.

It was introduced many years ago to stop games lasting too long. Before that, rallies used to be very long and one set could even last more than half an hour.

Nowadays, the expedite system is almost exclusively significant from a tactical point of view for defensive players, particularly if two defensive players are playing each other.

If two attacking players play each other, the time limit of 10 minutes is almost never reached; quite the reverse, as rallies at elite level are usually decided after the serve and one or two further shots. This is also, incidentally, one of the several reasons why our sport of table tennis is now rather lacking in spectators, and why for some time now, there have been attempts to make rallies longer by changing the rules. A few of these have been the introduction of larger 40 mm balls, the new scoring system, the new serving rules and the banning of speed glue.

Nevertheless, the discussion about this at national and international level still goes on.

Now take a look at point 15 of part A of the Rules on the subject of the Expedite System!

What are the tactical implications of the Expedite System?

As mentioned above, if you are an offensive player, it doesn't really affect you, unless you are playing a defensive player.

*If you are not really successful **attacking** but feel very confident playing push balls, then you can use this rule to your advantage!*

Simply push the ball back passively and then wait until the time runs out!

This forces the defender to take the initiative himself and to do what he is actually not so good at, i.e. attacking.

However, if he continues to play passively, time runs in your favor, provided that the set lasts longer than 10 minutes and that less than 18 points have been played. For then the expedite system comes into operation, in which the defensive player must become active when serving. Here you only need to return the ball 13 times in order to win a point.

ALSO:

Once introduced, the expedite system shall remain in operation until the end of the match. This also applies if the set lasts longer than 10 minutes without the expedite system coming into operation!

If two defensive players meet, the one with the better attacking game should try to bring the expedite system into operation!

He thereby relinquishes his initial advantage in order to be in a better position once the expedite system is implemented. For now both players must become active and this will be easier for the player with the better attacking game!

TABLE TENNIS RULES A

1 THE TABLE

1.1 The upper surface of the table, known as the playing surface, shall be rectangular, 2.74 m long and 1.525 m wide, and shall lie in a horizontal plane 76 cm above the floor.

1.2 The playing surface shall not include the vertical sides of the tabletop.

1.3 The playing surface may be of any material and shall yield a uniform bounce of about 23 cm when a standard ball is dropped on to it from a height of 30 cm.

1.4 The playing surface shall be uniformly dark coloured and matt, but with a white side line, 2 cm wide, along each 2.74 m edge and a white end line, 2 cm wide, along each 1.525 m edge.

1.5 The playing surface shall be divided into 2 equal courts by a vertical net running parallel with the end lines, and shall be continuous over the whole area of each court.

1.6 For doubles, each court shall be divided into 2 equal half-courts by a white centre line, 3 mm wide, running parallel with the side lines; the centre line shall be regarded as part of each right half-court.

2 THE NET ASSEMBLY

2.1 The net assembly shall consist of the net, its suspension and the supporting posts, including the clamps attaching them to the table.

2.2 The net shall be suspended by a cord attached at each end to an upright post 15.25 cm high, the outside limits of the post being 15.25 cm outside the side line.

2.3 The top of the net, along its whole length, shall be 15.25 cm above the playing surface.

2.4 The bottom of the net, along its whole length, shall be as close as possible to the playing surface and the ends of the net shall be attached to the supporting posts from top to bottom.

3 THE BALL

3.1 The ball shall be spherical, with a diameter of 40 mm.

3.2 The ball shall weigh 2.7 g.

3.3 The ball shall be made of celluloid or similar plastics material and shall be white or orange, and matt.

4 THE RACKET

4.1 The racket may be of any size, shape or weight but the blade shall be flat and rigid.

4.2 At least 85% of the blade by thickness shall be of natural wood; an adhesive layer within the blade may be reinforced with fibrous material such as carbon fibre, glass fibre or compressed paper, but shall not be thicker than 7.5% of the total thickness or 0.35 mm, whichever is the smaller.

4.3 A side of the blade used for striking the ball shall be covered with either ordinary pimpled rubber, with pimples outwards having a total thickness including adhesive of not more than 2.0 mm, or sandwich rubber, with pimples inwards or outwards, having a total thickness including adhesive of not more than 4.0 mm.

4.3.1 Ordinary pimpled rubber is a single layer of non-cellular rubber, natural or synthetic, with pimples evenly distributed over its surface at a density of not less than 10 per cm^2 and not more than 30 per cm^2.

4.3.2 Sandwich rubber is a single layer of cellular rubber covered with a single outer layer of ordinary pimpled rubber, the thickness of the pimpled rubber not being more than 2.0 mm.

4.4 The covering material shall extend up to but not beyond the limits of the blade, except that the part nearest the handle and gripped by the fingers may be left uncovered or covered with any material.

4.5 The blade, any layer within the blade and any layer of covering material or adhesive on a side used for striking the ball shall be continuous and of even thickness.

4.6 The surface of the covering material on a side of the blade, or of a side of the blade if it is left uncovered, shall be matt, bright red on one side and black on the other.

4.7 The racket covering shall be used without any physical, chemical or other treatment.

4.7.1 Slight deviations from continuity of surface or uniformity of colour due to accidental damage or wear may be allowed provided that they do not significantly change the characteristics of the surface.

4.8 Before the start of a match and whenever he or she changes his or her racket during a match a player shall show his or her opponent and the umpire the racket he or she is about to use and shall allow them to examine it.

5 DEFINITIONS

5.1 A rally is the period during which the ball is in play.

5.2 The ball is in play from the last moment at which it is stationary on the palm of the free hand before being intentionally projected in service until the rally is decided as a let or a point.

5.3 A let is a rally of which the result is not scored.

5.4 A point is a rally of which the result is scored.

5.5 The racket hand is the hand carrying the racket.

5.6 The free hand is the hand not carrying the racket; the free arm is the arm of the free hand.

5.7 A player strikes the ball if he or she touches it in play with his or her racket, held in the hand, or with his or her racket hand below the wrist.

5.8 A player obstructs the ball if he or she, or anything he or she wears or carries, touches it in play when it is above or travelling towards the playing surface, not having touched his or her court since last being struck by his or her opponent.

5.9 The server is the player due to strike the ball first in a rally.

5.10 The receiver is the player due to strike the ball second in a rally.

5.11 The umpire is the person appointed to control a match.

5.12 The assistant umpire is the person appointed to assist the umpire with certain decisions.

5.13 Anything that a player wears or carries includes anything that he or she was wearing or carrying, other than the ball, at the start of the rally.

5.14 The end line shall be regarded as extending indefinitely in both directions.

6 THE SERVICE

6.1 Service shall start with the ball resting freely on the open palm of the server's stationary free hand.

6.2 The server shall then project the ball near vertically upwards, without imparting spin, so that it rises at least 16cm after leaving the palm of the free hand and then falls without touching anything before being struck.

6.3 As the ball is falling the server shall strike it so that it touches first his or her court and then touches directly the receiver's court; in doubles, the ball shall touch successively the right half court of server and receiver.

6.4 From the start of service until it is struck, the ball shall be above the level of the playing surface and behind the server's end line, and it shall not be hidden from the receiver by the server or his or her doubles partner or by anything they wear or carry.

6.5 As soon as the ball has been projected, the server's free arm and hand shall be removed from the space between the ball and the net.

Note: The space between the ball and the net is defined by the ball, the net and its indefinite upward extension.

6.6 It is the responsibility of the player to serve so that the umpire or the assistant umpire can be satisfied that he or she complies with the requirements of the Laws, and either may decide that a service is incorrect.

6.6.1 If either the umpire or the assistant umpire is not sure about the legality of a service he or she may, on the first occasion in a match, interrupt play and warn the server; but any subsequent service by that player or his or her doubles partner which is not clearly legal shall be considered incorrect.

6.7 Exceptionally, the umpire may relax the requirements for a correct service where he or she is satisfied that compliance is prevented by physical disability.

7 THE RETURN

The ball, having been served or returned, shall be struck so that it touches the opponent's court, either directly or after touching the net assembly.

8 THE ORDER OF PLAY

8.1 In singles, the server shall first make a service, the receiver shall then make a return and thereafter server and receiver alternately shall each make a return.

8.2 In doubles, except as provided in 8.3, the server shall first make a service, the receiver shall then make a return, the partner of the server shall then make a return, the partner of the receiver shall then make a return and thereafter each player in turn in that sequence shall make a return.

8.3 In doubles, when at least one player of a pair is in a wheelchair due to a physical disability, the server shall first make a service, the receiver shall then make a return but thereafter either player of the disabled pair may make returns. However, no part of a player's wheelchair nor a foot of a standing player of this pair shall protrude beyond the imaginary extension of the centre line of the table. If it does, the umpire shall award the point to the opposing pair.

9 A LET

9.1 The rally shall be a let:

9.1.1 if in service the ball touches the net assembly, provided the service is otherwise correct or the ball is obstructed by the receiver or his or her partner;

9.1.2 if the service is delivered when the receiving player or pair is not ready, provided that neither the receiver nor his or her partner attempts to strike the ball;

9.1.3 if failure to make a service or a return or otherwise to comply with the Laws is due to a disturbance outside the control of the player;

9.1.4 if play is interrupted by the umpire or assistant umpire;

9.1.5 if the receiver is in wheelchair owing to a physical disability and in service the ball, provided that the service is otherwise correct,

9.1.5.1 after touching the receiver's court returns in the direction of the net;

9.1.5.2 comes to rest on the receiver's court;

9.1.5.3 in singles leaves the receiver's court after touching it by either of its sidelines.

9.2 Play may be interrupted:

9.2.1 to correct an error in the order of serving, receiving or ends;

9.2.2 to introduce the expedite system;

9.2.3 to warn or penalise a player or adviser;

9.2.4 because the conditions of play are disturbed in a way which could affect the outcome of the rally.

10 A POINT

10.1 Unless the rally is a let, a player shall score a point:

10.1.1 if an opponent fails to make a correct service;

10.1.2 if an opponent fails to make a correct return;

10.1.3 if, after he or she has made a service or a return, the ball touches anything other than the net assembly before being struck by an opponent;

10.1.4 if the ball passes over his or her court or beyond his or her end line without touching his or her court, after being struck by an opponent;

10.1.5 if the ball, after being struck by an opponent, passes through the net or between the net and the net post or between the net and playing surface;

10.1.6 if an opponent obstructs the ball;

10.1.7 if an opponent deliberately strikes the ball twice in succession;

10.1.8 if an opponent strikes the ball with a side of the racket blade whose surface does not comply with the requirements of 4.3, 4.4 and 4.5;

10.1.9 if an opponent, or anything an opponent wears or carries, moves the playing surface;

10.1.10 if an opponent, or anything an opponent wears or carries, touches the net assembly;

10.1.11 if an opponent's free hand touches the playing surface;

10.1.12 if a doubles opponent strikes the ball out of the sequence established by the first server and first receiver;

10.1.13 as provided under the expedite system (15.4).

10.1.14 if both players or pairs are in a wheelchair due to a physical disability and

10.1.14.1 his or her opponent does not maintain a minimum contact with the seat or cushion(s), with the back of the thigh, when the ball is struck;

10.1.14.2 his or her opponent touches the table with either hand before striking the ball;

10.1.14.3 his or her opponent's footrest or foot touches the floor during play.

10.1.15 as provided under the order of play (8.3).

11 A GAME

A game shall be won by the player or pair first scoring 11 points unless both players or pairs score 10 points, when the game shall be won by the first player or pair subsequently gaining a lead of 2 points.

12 A MATCH

12.1 A match shall consist of the best of any odd number of games.

13 THE ORDER OF SERVING, RECEIVING AND END

13.1 The right to choose the initial order of serving, receiving and ends shall be decided by lot and the winner may choose to serve or to receive first or to start at a particular end.

13.2 When one player or pair has chosen to serve or to receive first or to start at a particular end, the other player or pair shall have the other choice.

13.3 After each 2 points have been scored the receiving player or pair shall become the serving player or pair and so on until the end of the game, unless both players or pairs score 10 points or the expedite system is in operation, when the sequences of serving and receiving shall be the same but each player shall serve for only 1 point in turn.

13.4 In each game of a doubles match, the pair having the right to serve first shall choose which of them will do so and in the first game of a match the receiving pair shall decide which of them will receive first; in subsequent games of the match, the first server having been chosen, the first receiver shall be the player who served to him or her in the preceding game.

13.5 In doubles, at each change of service the previous receiver shall become the server and the partner of the previous server shall become the receiver.

13.6 The player or pair serving first in a game shall receive first in the next game of the match and in the last possible game of a doubles match the pair due to receive next shall change their order of receiving when first one pair scores 5 points.

13.7 The player or pair starting at one end in a game shall start at the other end in the next game of the match and in the last possible game of a match the players or pairs shall change ends when first one player or pair scores 5 points.

14 OUT OF ORDER OF SERVING, RECEIVING OR ENDS

14.1 If a player serves or receives out of turn, play shall be interrupted by the umpire as soon as the error is discovered and shall resume with those players serving and receiving who should be server and receiver respectively at the score that has been reached, according to the sequence established at the beginning of the match and, in doubles, to the order of serving chosen by the pair having the right to serve first in the game during which the error is discovered.

14.2 If the players have not changed ends when they should have done so, play shall be interrupted by the umpire as soon as the error is discovered and shall resume with the players at the ends at which they should be at the score that has been reached, according to the sequence established at the beginning of the match.

14.3 In any circumstances, all points scored before the discovery of an error shall be reckoned.

15 THE EXPEDITE SYSTEM

15.1 Except as provided in 15.2, the expedite system shall come into operation after 10 minutes' play in a game or at any time when requested by both players or pairs.

15.2 The expedite system shall not be introduced in a game if at least 18 points have been scored.

15.3 If the ball is in play when the time limit is reached and the expedite system is due to come into operation, play shall be interrupted by the umpire and shall resume with service by the player who served in the rally that was interrupted; if the ball is not in play when the expedite system comes into operation, play shall resume with service by the player who received in the immediately preceding rally.

15.4 Thereafter, each player shall serve for 1 point in turn until the end of the game, and if the receiving player or pair makes 13 correct returns in a rally the receiver shall score a point.

15.5 Introduction of the expedite system shall not alter the order of serving and receiving in the match, as defined in 13.6.

15.6 Once introduced, the expedite system shall remain in operation until the end of the match.

FINAL QUESTIONNAIRE

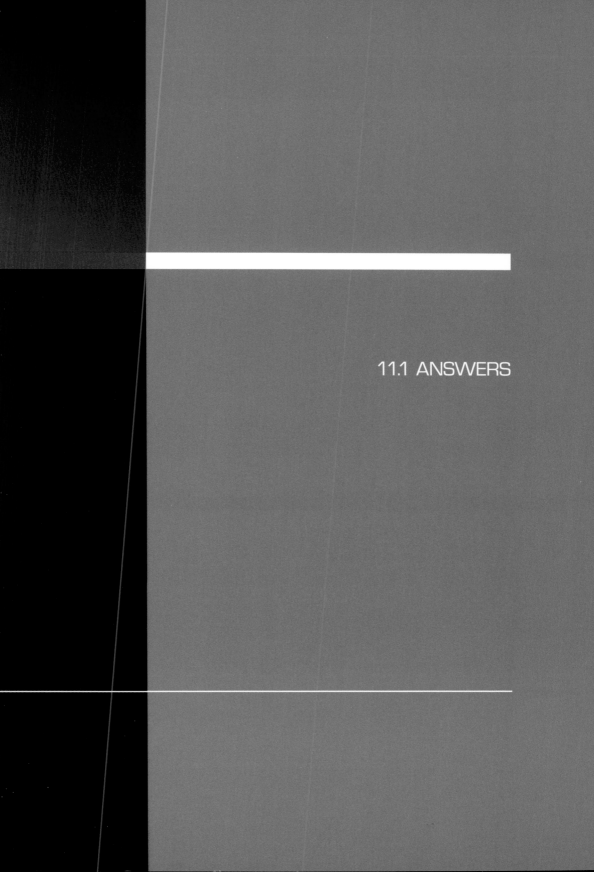

11.1 ANSWERS

11 FINAL QUESTIONNAIRE

1. The player who decides to receive serve after winning the right to choose at the start of the first set:

a) serves at the end of the second, fourth and if applicable at the end of the sixth and seventh sets (9:9, 10:8, 8:10).

b) receives serve at the end of the first, third and if applicable at the end of the fifth or seventh sets.

c) serves at the end of the first, third and if applicable at the end of the fifth or seventh sets.

d) gains no influence thereby over whether he serves or receives serve at the end of the sets.

2. Which sentence is correct?

   Slow, high topspins tend to be blocked out of the table more often than fast, flat topspins

a) because slow, high topspins usually have more spin than fast, flat topspins.

b) because due to the higher angle of incidence on the table, the ball also bounces higher than is the case for a flat topspin.

3. Is it possible to return a ball with heavy backspin with another ball with backspin when hitting with an anti-topspin surface?

a) Yes.

b) No.

4. Which sentence is correct?

   The 'elbow' placing point of a BH dominant player is usually found

a) exactly in the middle of the table.

b) Further to the backhand side than for a FH dominant player.

c) Further to the forehand side than for a FH dominant player.

5. Heavy spin cannot be produced with short pips.

a) Correct.

b) Incorrect.

6. If a topspin (with a lot of spin) is blocked with long pips, this block is returned with

a) topspin.

b) backspin.

c) no spin.

7. Which sentence is correct?

   Playing to the deep forehand of a FH dominant player is

a) tactically unwise, as his forehand will usually be much better than his backhand.

b) tactically wise, as he usually has problems with this placing.

8. Which sentence is correct?

Against heavy backspin one can

a) play a smash, even if the ball does not bounce higher than net height and thereby attain a good strike rate (more than 50 %).

b) in general not smash and thereby attain a good strike rate (more than 50%).

c) play a smash, but only if the ball bounces higher than net height.

9. Which sentence is correct?

Good flip players can usually flip harder and more confidently

a) short balls with slight topspin.

b) short balls with little backspin.

c) short balls with heavy backspin.

10. With which hitting point of the racket does a forehand serve with good wrist action give the ball most spin?

a)

b)

c)

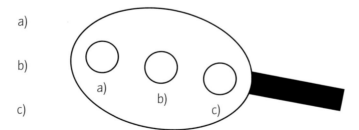

11. Which sentence is correct?

    The more topspin a ball has

a) the more curved its trajectory.

b) the flatter its trajectory.

c) the topspin has no affect on the trajectory of the ball. The only determining factor is how hard the ball is hit.

12. Which sentence is correct?

    A forehand sidespin can be hit with a BH grip

a) more easily

b) less easily

c) equally easily

    as with a FH grip.

13. Which sentence is correct?

    With a FH grip one can

a) change quickly from the forehand to the backhand.

b) change quickly from the backhand to the forehand.

c) not change sides quickly at all.

14. Which sentence is correct?

A high racket grip

a)   reduces wrist mobility during short net play.

b)   has a big advantage (more control) in long actions.

c)   both the above points are correct.

d)   has no effect on the control of individual shots.

15. Which of the following strokes can be used to return a FH topspin with the greatest topspin?

a)   hard/strong backspin defensive shot.

b)   block.

c)   weak/gentle push ball.

11.1   ANSWERS

Question 1   c   see "The choice of serving, receiving and ends" (8.1)

Question 2   b   see "Flight height—general" (3.1) and "Producing Spin" (4.1)

Question 3   b   see "Antis" (4.4.1.1)

Question 4   c   see "Characteristics of a backhand dominant player" (1.4.2)

Question 5   b   see "Short Pips" (4.4.2.1)

Question 6   b   see "Long Pips" (4.4.2.2)

Question 7   b   see "Tips for playing against forehand dominant players" (1.4.1.1)

Question 8   a   see "Backspin" (4.2.1)

Question 9   c   see "Backspin" (4.2.1)

Question 10   a   see "Service Feints with/without spin" (5.1.1)

Question 11   a   see "Rules of Thumb for identifying spin" (4.2)

Question 12   a   see "Grip Table according to Östh & Felke" (1.3.1)

Question 13   b   see "Grip Table according to Östh & Felke" (1.3.1)

Question 14   c   see "Racket Grip" (1.3)

Question 15   a   see "Topspin" (4.2.2)

PROFILES OF A FEW FORMER AND CURRENT TABLE TENNIS STARS

12 PROFILES OF A FEW FORMER AND CURRENT TABLE TENNIS STARS

12.1

Name:	Timo Boll
Date of Birth:	March 8th 1981
Place of Birth:	Erbach, Germany
Hobbies:	Golf, diving, reading, Internet
Current club:	Borussia Düsseldorf
Career Highlights:	Olympic Silver with the team in Beijing, 2008 Olympic Bronze with the team in London 2012, 2016 Six-time European Champion 2002, 2007, 2008, 2010, 2011, 2012 Winner Grand Finals singles and doubles 2005 World Championships doubles runner up (with C. Süß) 2005 World Cup winner 2005, 2002 World Championships runner up with the team 2004, 2010, 2012, 2014 First German to be ranked world #1 in January 2003 World Championships Bronze 2011 European singles and doubles champion 2002 Many times German Champion
Blade:	Butterfly "Timo Boll ALC OFF"
FH rubber:	Butterfly "Tenergy 05" 2.1 mm
BH rubber:	Butterfly "Tenergy 05" 2.1 mm
Game:	Offensive player with heavy FH and BH topspin. Left-hander.

12.2

Name:	Vladimir Samsonov
Date of Birth:	April 14th 1976
Place of Birth:	Minsk (Belarus)
Hobbies:	Cinema, Music
Current club:	Fakel Orenburg
Career Highlights:	Table Tennis World Cup champion with Villette Charleroi 2004, 2006 European champion 2005, 2003, 1997 World Cup winner 2009, 2001, 1999 World Championships runner-up 1997
Blade:	Tibhar "Samsonov Alpha"
FH rubber:	Tibhar "Nimbus VIP"
BH rubber:	Tibhar "Nimbus VIP"
Game:	Very flexible all-around game. Very good ball control. Right-hander.

12.3

Name:	Ma Long
Date of birth:	October 20th 1988
Place of birth:	Liaoning, PR China
Career highlights:	Olympic Champion 2016
	Olympic Team Champion 2012, 2016
	World Champion 2015
	Team World Champion 2006, 2008, 2010, 2012, 2014, 2016
	Asian Cup men's finalist 2008, 2009
Blade:	Double Happiness, TG-7 BL
FH rubber:	Double Happiness, Dipper 2.2 mm
BH rubber:	Double Happiness, Dipper 2.2 mm
Game:	Attacking. Shakehand grip. Right-hander.

12.4

Name:	Fan Zhendong
Date of birth:	January 22th 1997
Place of birth:	Guangzhou
Career highlights:	World Champion with the team 2014, 2016
Blade:	STIGA „Infinity YPS V"
FH rubber:	DHS „Neo Hurricane III" 2.1 mm
BH rubber:	DHS „Calibra Tour M" 2.1 mm
Game:	Shakehand-grip player. Right-hander with attacking style using explosive footwork and thunderous forehand loops to finish off his opponents.

12.5

Name:	Jun Mizutani
Date of birth:	June 9th 1989
Place of birth:	Iwata, Japan
Career highlight:	Winner of the Korean Open 2009 Winner of the Bronze Medal Olympic Games 2016 Winner of the Japan Open 2012
Blade:	Butterfly „Mizutani Jun ST"
FH rubber:	Butterfly „Tenergy-64" 2.1 mm
BH rubber:	Butterfly „Tenergy-64" 2.1 mm
Game:	Offensive. Shakehand grip. Left-hander.

12.6

Name:	Dimitriy Ovtcharov
Date of Birth:	September 2nd 1988
Place of Birth:	Kiev (Ukraine)
Hobbies:	Pool, cinema, music
Current club:	Fakel Gazproma Orenburg, Russia
Career Highlights:	Olympic team silver in Beijing, 2008 Olympic team bronze in London, 2012, 2016 European team Champion 2006 and 2008 European Champion 2013, 2015 European Junior team Champion 2006 European Junior Champion 2005 Top of European Junior rankings 2005
Blade:	Donic "Waldner Senso Carbon"
FH rubber:	Donic "Coppa Speed" 2.1 mm
BH rubber:	Donic "Coppa Speed" 2.1 mm
Game:	Offensive player with surprise changes of pace and spin. Very good serve. Right-hander.

12.7

Name:	Michael Maze
Date of birth:	September 1st 1981
Place of birth:	Fakse, Denmark
Career highlights:	European men's singles champion in 2009 Team European champion in 2005 Olympic doubles bronze medalist in 2004 (with Tugwell) World men's singles bronze medalist in 2005
Blade:	Butterfly „Maze Passion OFF-"
FH rubber:	Butterfly „Bryce-Speed" 2.1 mm
BH rubber:	Butterfly „Tenergy-05" 2.1 mm
Game:	Offensive. Left-hander.

12.8

Name:	Werner Schlager
Date of Birth:	September 28th 1972
Place of Birth:	Wiener Neustadt (Austria)
Hobby:	Computer
Current club:	SVS Niederösterreich
Career Highlights:	World Champion 2003 European Doubles Champion 2005 Winner Top 12 Europe 2000, 2008
Blade:	Butterfly "Schlager Carbon OFF+"
FH subber:	Butterfly "Tenergy 05" 2.1 mm
BH rubber:	Butterfly "Tenergy 05" 2.1 mm
Game:	Offensive player with extremely good ball control. Intelligent tactician. Right-hander.

12.9

Name:	Joo Se Hyuk
Date of birth:	January 20th 1980
Place of birth:	Seoul, South Korea
Career highlight:	World Championships men's singles runner-up 2003
Blade:	Butterfly „Joo Se Hyuk DEF"
FH rubber:	Butterfly „Tenergy-64" 2.1 mm
BH rubber:	TSP „Curl P1"
Game:	Defensive (considered to be the best defensive player in the world). Right-hander.

12.10

Name:	Jan-Ove Waldner
Date of Birth:	October 3rd 1965
Place of Birth:	Fittja (Sweden)
Hobbies:	Golf, dice, horse racing, cinema
Current club:	Spårvägens BTK, Sweden
Career Highlights:	Olympic Champion 1992 Barcelona World Champion 1989 and 1997 Olympic Semi-finalist 2004 Has influenced international table tennis for more than two decades. 2016 career end
Blade:	Donic "Waldner Senso Carbon"
FH rubber:	Donic "Coppa JO Gold"
BH rubber:	Donic "Coppa JO Platin"
Game:	"The greatest player of all time." "The Mozart of table tennis." Flexible attacking game with very good service and well-placed topspins as well as hard blocks and smashes. Constantly includes surprise shots, such as backspin blocks. Right-hander.

12.11

Name:	Wang Hao
Date of birth:	December 15th 1983
Place of birth:	Changchun, PR China
Career Highlights:	World men's singles and doubles champion 2009 World Championships runner up 2011, 2013 Olympic team champion 2008, 2012 World team champion 2004, 2006, 2008, 2010, 2012, 2014 2014 career end
Blade:	Double Happiness, Hurricane
FH rubber:	Double Happiness, NEO Skyline III 2.1 mm
BH rubber:	Double Happiness, NEO Skyline III 2.1 mm
Game:	Penhold grip with reverse penhold backhand, right-hander, attacking player.

12.12

Name:	Wang Liqin
Date of birth:	June 18th 1978
Place of birth:	Shanghai, PR China
Career highlights:	Olympic team champion 2008 in Bejing World champion 2001, 2005, 2007 World team champion 2000, 2001, 2001, 2006, 2008 2013 career end
Blade:	Double Happiness, Hurricane King
FH rubber:	Double Happiness, NEO Hurricane II 2.1 mm
BH rubber:	Double Happiness, NEO Hurricane III 2.1 mm
Game:	Shakehand grip, right-hander, attacking player.

12.13

Name:	Ma Lin
Date of birth:	February 19th 1980
Place of birth:	Shenyang, PR China
Career highlights:	Olympic Champion 2008 in Bejing Olympic Team Champion 2008 in Bejing World team champion 2001, 2004, 2006, 2008, 2010, 2012 2013 career end
Blade:	Yasaka Ma Lin Carbon Off
FH rubber:	Double Happiness Skyline 2.2 mm
BH rubber:	Butterfly Bryce 2.1 mm
Game:	Offensive penhold player with reverse penhold backhand, right-hander.

12.14

Name:	Petrissa Solja
Date of birth:	March 11th 1994
Place of birth:	Kandel, Germany
Career highlights:	TTC Berlin Eastside Olympic Silver with the team 2016 European Champion with the team 2013,2014, 2015 German women's singles and doubles (with Winter) champion in 2015
Blade:	JOOLA „Rosskopf Emotion"
FH rubber:	JOOLA Rhyzm-P max.
BH rubber:	JOOLA Rhyzm-P max.
Game:	Offensive player. Left-hander.

12.15

Name:	Elizabeta Samara
Date of birth:	April 15th 1989
Place of birth:	Constanta, Romania
Career highlights:	European women's doubles champion in 2009 (with Dodean)
Blade:	Tibhar "Samsonov Premium Contact"
FH rubber:	Tibhar „Sinus" max.
BH rubber:	Tibhar „Nianmor" max.
Game:	Left-hander. Offensive player.

12.16

Name:	Daniela Dodean
Date of birth:	January 13th 1988
Place of birth:	Arad, Romania
Career highlights:	European women's doubles champion (with Samara)
	European women's junior champion 2005 and 2006
Blade:	Butterfly „Primorac-Carbon-FL"
FH rubber:	Butterfly „Tenergy-05" 2.1 mm
BH rubber:	Butterfly „Tenergy-64" 2.1 mm
Game:	Attacking player. Right-hander.

12.17

Name:	Guo Yue
Date of birth:	July 17th 1988
Place of birth:	Anshan, PR China
Career highlights:	World Champion 2007 World team champion 2004, 2006, 2008, 2009, 2012 Olympic team champion 2008, 2012 2014 career end
Blade:	Butterfly Special Made (Blade) FL
FH rubber:	DHS „Hurricane" 2.0 mm
BH rubber:	Butterfly „Tenergy-64" 2.1 mm
Game:	Left-hander. Attacking player.

12.18

Name:	Zhang Yining
Date of birth:	October 5th 1982
Place of birth:	Beijing, PR China
Career highlights:	Olympic women's singles & team champion 2008 World Champion 2009 Olympic women's singles and doubles (with Wang Nan) champion in 2004 2011 career end
Blade:	Butterfly Special Made (Innerforce) FL
FH rubber:	Butterfly „Tenergy-05" 2.1 mm
BH rubber:	Butterfly „Tenergy-64" 2.1 mm
Game:	Attacking player. Shakehand grip. Right-hander.

PHOTO CREDITS

Cover design:	Andreas Reuel
Cover photo:	© picture-alliance/dpa
Interior layout:	Claudia Sakyi
Interior photos:	Guido Schuchert, Butterfly; Andro; Tibar, Donic
	© imago-sportfotodienst
	(page 13, 85, 95, 141)
	© picture alliance
	(page 165, 175)
Graphics and Illustrations:	Oliver Sprigade, Hanover, Germany
Typesetting:	www.satzstudio-hilger.de
Editing:	Anne Rumery, Kristina Oltrogge

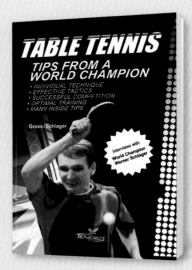

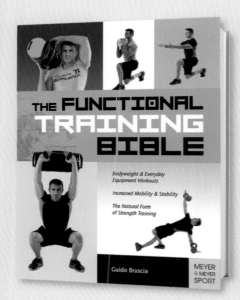

Guido Bruscia

THE FUNCTIONAL TRAINING BIBLE

512 p., 7.7″ x 10″, in color
657 photos, 26 illus.
paperback
ISBN 9781782550457

$ 24.95 US/$ 49.95 AUS
£ 19.95 UK/€ 24.95

Functional training is easy, fast and fun. The book is divided into three parts: The theoretical part explains the 'why' at the foundation of functional training; the practical part contains bodyweight exercises and exercises with various tools (sandbags, medicine ball, kettlebells). The final section proposes several specific training programs.

MEYER & MEYER Sport
Von-Coels-Str. 390
52080 Aachen
Germany

Phone   +49 02 41 - 9 58 10 - 13
Fax   +49 02 41 - 9 58 10 - 10
E-Mail   sales@m-m-sports.com
Website www.m-m-sports.com

All books available as E-books.

MEYER
& MEYER
SPORT